I0796945

The MOSAIC of the DIVINE SYMPHONY

The MOSAIC of the DIVINE SYMPHONY

Legacy of Faith in the Land of Promise

Ellen Y. Yan
阎颖

Carpenter's Son Publishing

The Mosaic of the Divine Symphony: Legacy of Faith in the Land of Promise

Published by Carpenter's Son Publishing, Franklin, TN
Christianbookservices.com

Cover and Interior Design by Suzanne Lawing

Cover Photo by Bing Liang

Printed in the United States of America

ISBN: 978-1-956370-73-7 (print)

ACKNOWLEDGMENTS

This book was called into being by God, and by His grace it has come to completion. To Him be all the glory.

I extend my heartfelt gratitude to Rev. David Chow, the eldest son of Rev. Moses Chow, for his invaluable contributions about his father and his meticulous insights throughout this book. His contributions have been indispensable to this book.

I am also deeply grateful to Mr. Richard Choy—the eldest son of Rev. Ted Choy and Leona Choy—and Dr. Ivan Leaman, whose ancestors were cousins of the Leaman family at Leaman Place. Their vital contributions have enriched this book immensely.

I am thankful to AFC for providing the founders' biographies, connecting me with Leona, and sharing precious historic Leaman family photos.

My deepest appreciation goes to Mrs. Leona Choy, the last surviving founder of AFC, whose mentorship and guidance were critical to my finishing the book. She referred me to Carpenter's Son Publishing, whose instrumental assistance has been vital in bringing this book to fruition.

I am profoundly thankful to my family—Bing, Reece, and Mina Liang—for their unwavering support throughout this spiritual journey. Their own journeys of faith are shared in the epilogue.

May this book be used by God to enlighten those who seek to understand His works in the past and to remain attuned to His ongoing guidance in our lives.

TABLE OF CONTENTS

EPILOGUE: THE SPIRITUAL JOURNEY OF THE LIANGS

PREFACE

Dear Readers,

As I begin to share the inspiring stories of missionaries connected with the Leaman Family in Leaman Place, the land dubbed the "Land of Promise" by the English Quaker William Penn, I am filled with awe and reverence for the living God who has moved so powerfully in their lives. These narratives, associated with Ambassadors for Christ, Inc. (AFC), a major Christian organization in North America, bear witness to God's enduring presence and influence. This book is not merely a collection of historical accounts; it is a testament to the unwavering power and presence of God, who continues to work mightily in the hearts of those who serve Him.

The unwavering faith and dedication of the missionaries depicted in this book have carried the light of the gospel to the farthest corners of the earth. Their lives form a vivid tapestry, woven with threads of courage, sacrifice, and divine intervention. Through their stories, we witness God's fingerprints, marvel at His provision, and stand in awe of His unchanging love.

A profound theme that emerges from these accounts is the importance of spiritual inheritance. The heritage of the missionaries reminds us of the crucial task of passing our faith to future generations. Their faithfulness impacted not only their immediate circles but have also laid a foundation for the spiritual journeys of countless others.

This powerful legacy urges us to nurture and guide our offspring in the ways of the Lord.

As you journey through these pages, feel the heartbeat of history and the pulse of the present, intertwined in the living tapestry of God's enduring presence. The same God who guided their steps, whispered in their hearts, and illuminated their paths is here with us now, calling us to be His vessels of light in a world that yearns for His touch.

May these accounts stir your spirit, filling you with courage and hope, as you realize the sacred duty we share—to carry forward this flame of faith. Feel the weight of this responsibility, but also the joy, knowing that you are part of an unbroken chain of believers who have trusted in God's unfailing guidance. Let the legacy of these missionaries inspire you to recognize God's active presence in your own life, urging you to respond to His call with unwavering faith and obedience.

And as you do, remember the generations that follow. Just as those before us passed down the torch of faith, it is now our turn to ensure that its light burns brightly in the hearts of those who come after us. May this book not only inspire you but also equip you to be a beacon of hope and a carrier of this divine heritage, so that the story of God's love and faithfulness continues to unfold through the ages.

With every page, may you draw closer to the living God who is as present and powerful today as He was with the missionaries of the nineteenth century.

AUTHOR'S BACKGROUND

I was born in Tianjin, China, into an academic family where both of my parents were college professors. My formative years were engulfed by the notorious Chinese Cultural Revolution, during which my family was relocated to a small and remote village to work as farmers. This upheaval concluded during my teenage years.

My adolescence years were spent at Tianjin Nankai Middle School, a prestigious institution known for its illustrious alumni, including Premiers Zhou Enlai and Wen Jiabao. I pursued my undergraduate studies at the People's University of China and continued with graduate studies at Nankai University. The nurturing environment at home and the rigorous training at school provided a solid foundation for my future.

In 1988, at the age of 24, I journeyed to the United States to pursue a Ph.D. in Economics at the University of Iowa. The following year, I married my husband, Bing Liang, who was then a Ph.D. student in Finance. In 1991, we welcomed our son, Reece, into the world. After earning my Ph.D. in 1996, I spent over ten years building a career in the financial industry before founding my own financial consulting company. Despite my professional endeavors, writing has remained an enduring passion, and many of my works have been published in Chinese Christian magazines.

Before coming to the United States, I had no religious background, nor did my parents or grandparents. My journey of faith began in my mid-thirties, about ten years after my arrival in the United States. Having met the challenges of establishing my career and family, I found my soul yearning for something beyond professional success and familial fulfillment.

Embracing faith was a challenging and gradual journey for me. The lingering effects of the Chinese Cultural Revolution made it difficult to trust, especially after experiencing betrayal by those we once considered friends. Believing in something so intangible was even harder. However, through profound spiritual encounters with God, these barriers began to fall away.

In 2000, my entire family was baptized into Christianity, and four months later, my daughter Mina was born. The Thanksgiving Christian conferences in Chicago and the Agape Renewal Ministry in California became pivotal in guiding us, awakening our hearts to the presence of the Holy Spirit, and kindling a deep yearning for spiritual encounters. We experienced God's profound presence woven into the fabric of our lives, and this writing project serves as a testament to how God works through us, guiding us to fulfill His divine purpose.

THE DIVINE CALLING

On the morning of November 1, 2020, as I jogged along tranquil trails as my daily routine, my thoughts turned to my five-year home-schooling journey with my daughter, Mina. I envisioned writing a book that would help parents facing the challenges brought on by the COVID-19 pandemic.

However, during that quiet reflection, I felt a profound spiritual calling to document the stories of early missionaries who dedicated their lives to the Chinese people, as well as the founders of prominent Chinese Christian organizations. This divine directive was daunting—my educational background was in financial economics, I had little knowledge of missionary history, and English was my second language.

With a heart full of humility, I prayed, "Lord, I am ready to follow Your lead. This task is beyond my capacity, but I surrender to Your will. Please guide me, for I do not know whom to contact, what to write, or how to write it."

As I embarked on this journey, God brought key figures into my life, including Mrs. Leona Choy, co-founder of Ambassadors for Christ (AFC). She became a spiritual mother and mentor, nurturing my writing and guiding me through the challenges of publishing in English.

When Leona passed away on March 2, 2023, I was left feeling lost and unmotivated, as if the project had lost its heart. My work came to a standstill, and I prayed earnestly, asking, "Lord, this is Your project. What do You want me to do with it? Who is my target reader? Who will care about the missionaries who dedicated their lives to the

Chinese, especially now that China is seen as a rival to the U.S.?" For months, I received no clear answer.

In this period of struggling, I came across Pastor Jian Zhu's class, "God's Fingerprint." A second-generation Chinese pastor from mainland China, Pastor Zhu possessed deep insights into the workings of the Holy Spirit, and I felt he might be able to give me some clues. After attending his class and meeting with him one-on-one, I shared my struggles about my calling.

Pastor Zhu offered me two pieces of advice that were crucial: "First, reflect on whether you've deviated from God's original plan. Can you distinguish between divine inspiration and human inspiration? Though they can be difficult to tell apart, they are different. Second, remember that God might use this project to bless others and lead you to something new. Writing this book might not be your ultimate destination, but rather a milestone. Once you finish, God may open new doors for you."

His words were a revelation. I realized that I had been so fixated on this book that I couldn't see beyond it. With renewed inspiration from his wisdom, I picked up my pen once more and wrote tirelessly, day and night, to complete the book.

All glory be to God, who sends His angels, like Mrs. Leona Choy and Pastor Jian Zhu, to guide us when we are lost and cannot see the path ahead. Once I resolved to finish this book, it was as if the "Jordan waters" parted before me, allowing me to cross smoothly and complete the work.

Foreword 1

FROM MISSIONARY JOURNAL TO MISSIONARY JOURNEY

A book may inspire us all to participate in a new era of world missions

Pastor Jian Zhu

When I first met Ellen and her husband, Bing, I was struck by their impressive achievements as professionals, their dedication to community service, and their active involvement in Christian ministries in the United States. By cultural standards, they had realized the American Dream. However, along their journey, they encountered Jesus, and in Him, they discovered a purpose far beyond worldly success.

Pastor Jian Zhu

At the time, Ellen and Bing were both students in my "Devotion and Knowing God's Fingerprints" training course—a program I have developed, practiced, and taught for nearly 40 years. This course has been well-received among Chinese churches and Christian communities for decades. When we met, the couple was earnestly pursuing a higher calling from God, driven by a deep passion to serve Him.

Ellen's first counseling session with me centered on a book she felt called to write—a historical account of missionaries. Although she had no prior experience or direction for such a project, she was unwavering in her conviction that God had called her to this task. Through my comprehensive process of discerning and interpreting God's will, I recognized that her journey mirrored the teachings from my course on God's fingerprints. I believed I could help her understand and follow the Holy Spirit's leading.

It was evident that Ellen's decision to embark on this book-writing journey—an endeavor that closely resembled an anthropological study of Ambassadors for Christ (AFC)—was far outside the realm of her usual experiences. This unfamiliar territory understandably left her puzzled.

Given my background in applied anthropology from the University of New Mexico and over 20 years in Christian ministry among Chinese Mainlanders, I understood Ellen's deeper questions: Why was she chosen for this task? Why this book? And why write it in English?

After my initial conversation with Ellen and her husband Bing, I had the opportunity to observe Ellen's journey over several months as she sought to understand and follow God's will. It became increasingly clear to me that her passion and determination to write this historical account of Ambassadors for Christ (AFC) was indeed inspired by the Holy Spirit—a divine assignment from God.

However, as I followed her progress, I realized that God's purpose for Ellen extended far beyond simply uncovering, compiling, and sharing these seemingly forgotten missionary stories. The lives of those who dedicated and sacrificed themselves for the Gospel planted seeds of God's love in the hearts and cultures of nations. These stories must be watered, nurtured, retold, and lived out so that each of us might discover the meaning, honor, and passionate hope that comes from living for God's higher purpose. This is especially significant for

Christians from Mainland China, who may need these stories of selfless dedication to wash away generational suffering and pain, allowing them to experience God's love in a way that heals, transforms, and empowers.

Ellen's personal journey, along with her family's, demonstrates that writing this book about the legacy of AFC carries deep significance. It is not just about preserving history; it is about passing on the mission and mantle of AFC to future generations. I humbly acknowledge that I have known of AFC's ministry for decades, and both I and the ministry organization I lead have greatly benefited from our partnership with them.

Still important questions remain: Why write this book in English? Who are the intended readers? If Ellen and Bing's life journey is representative of many Christians from Mainland China, then it is time for the global Mainland Chinese Christian diaspora to rise up and take on their responsibilities as God's children. They must explore, learn, experience, and share these stories with the broader family of God's Kingdom.

This book carries three distinctive characteristics that trace the stories of past missionary heroes through the lens of AFC: First, it is a historical account of lifelong missionaries who, though they may seem distant, remain close to us in spirit and impact. Second, it highlights God's fingerprints, connecting the dots to show how His servants continue to influence our lives today. Third, it serves as a unique and rare anthropological study, offering valuable insights, particularly to Chinese Mainlanders and those who wish to understand the spiritual and life transformation of this community. In this context, Ellen's work stands out as an exemplary case.

With these reflections in mind, I pray that as you read these stories, you will see how the lives of past Christian missionaries have not only transformed many but also how, through Ellen—representative of her generation of Chinese Mainlanders—their heartbeats, sighs, tears, and passion for God are woven into every word and line of this book.

May God's will continue to be done among His people, just as it was in previous generations, and as it will be in the generations to come.

Pastor Jian Zhu co-founded America's first Mainland Chinese Christian church following China's opening in the 1980s. He also co-founded the North America Mainland Chinese Mission (NAMCM), serving as its first President (2000-2003) and now as Permanent Vice President. Additionally, he co-founded America China Civic Exchange, leading as Chief Executive for over 20 years.

In 1983, while in Wuhan, China, Pastor Zhu and his fellow ministry workers were given a vision of twin missions—an evangelical mandate and a socio-cultural mandate. For over 40 years, Pastor Zhu has remained steadfast in pursuing this vision, helping to establish Mainland Chinese ministries around the world. His wife, Rebecca, serves alongside him as a pastor, and their son Samuel, a campus minister, founded an Asian chapter of InterVarsity at North Carolina State University.

Foreword 2

HARVESTING A LEGACY OF FAITH

Dr. Yeou Cherng Bor, the President of AFC

Dr. Yeou Cherng Bor

Friendship shines a light more brightly on the inner workings of ministry because both find their home in the heart. The friendship of Ellen Yan with Leona Choy sparks just such a light. Leona Choy is so centrally foundational to Ambassadors for Christ (AFC) that to connect with her is to connect with a vital part of the heart of the ministry. The friendship of Ellen and Leona gives us a unique vantage into this ministry that was so close to Leona's heart.

About the ministry of Ambassadors for Christ, Mrs. Leona Choy wrote,

> *"It is easy to plant the seed of a fragile ornamental flower. However, when you want to grow a sturdy oak tree, you plant a small acorn and patiently wait year after year, even generation after generation, to see the results of your planting. You may not live to see the mature massive strong oak it will become. Decades*

later in the future others may benefit from its shade and wood harvested from its trunk for building great structure."

—Leona Choy, The Blessed Journey,
Celebrating AFC's Half-Century.

In the 1960s, Leona Choy, her husband Ted Choy, and Moses Chow, with the encouragement of Christiana Tsai, planted that "acorn" for Christ. Perhaps, little did they dream of what it would become six decades later. AFC has grown into a hardy "oak tree" spreading its branches across at least three continents. These founders received from God a strategic vision: reaching Chinese intellectuals for Christ in this generation. This vision remains unchanged. They left behind a rich legacy and role model that will continue to inspire AFC to stay on course, winning Chinese intellectuals and cultivating them into disciples of Jesus Christ.

We can read about organizations and look at charts, but to know the heart of a ministry we must get to know the people. From Charles Leaman to Mary Leaman, Christiana Tsai, Ted and Leona Choy, and Moses Chow, these pillars behind the ministry of Ambassadors for Christ had a deep love for the Lord and for Chinese people around the world. It was their desire for Chinese to come to know Christ and be a vital missionary force for God's Kingdom. Ellen graciously tells their stories and their passion with enthusiasm, love, and respect.

Every morning when I walk into the AFC building, I cannot help but think when Charles Leaman set foot on Chinese soil in 1874, he probably never imagined that 150 years later, in his hometown of Paradise, PA, there would be an evangelical organization that continues his ministry, proclaiming the gospel of Jesus Christ to Chinese intellectuals in the United States and beyond. What Charles Leaman, Mary Leaman, Christiana Tsai, Ted and Leona Choy, and Moses Chow imagined is growing up through the ministry of AFC. Out of a humble farm property generously donated by people who saw the vision, grew a ministry that reaches to the hearts of the largest people group in the world.

AFC is committed to strategically sending campus missionaries to select university campuses in the United States; reaching and walking with graduates who just started their careers; and cultivating young couples to commit to local churches as faithful members of the body of Christ. In a nutshell, AFC will form a strong partnership with Chinese immigrant churches in North America to reach 18-38 year-old, Mandarin-speaking intellectuals with the Gospel of Jesus Christ, including international students, young professionals, and young families. Ultimately, this young generation will be transformed into disciples of Jesus Christ and continue to multiply for generations to come in a global setting.

In 1 Corinthians 3:6-7, Paul exhorted the church at Corinth to be mindful of why they existed as the body of Christ. He writes, "*I planted, Apollos watered, but God gave them growth. So neither he who plants nor he who waters is anything, but only God who gives the growth*" (ESV). The staff members of AFC fully understand that it is by the grace of God, and His grace only, that the "acorns" AFC planted and watered have been able to grow into "oak trees." Paul reminds us of who we are individually and corporately in the body of Christ: we are His ambassadors entrusted with this glorious ministry and message to point people to Christ, the Savior who reconciles us with God through His perfect redemption and resurrection. Together, let us press on, continuing to build His kingdom on the Cornerstone, which is Jesus Christ, by taking the message of the Gospel to the world and equipping those who commit to walk the path that leads to His glorious kingdom.

We are grateful to Ellen Yan for her efforts in compiling these stories together to encourage a new generation of believers to follow the Lord where He leads, plant the "acorns" where He wants us to plant them, and then let the Lord grow them into marvelous oak trees for His honor and glory!

The President of Ambassadors for Christ, Inc.
Paradise, PA

Dr. Yeou Cherng Bor, originally from Taiwan, earned his Ph.D. in industrial microbiology and molecular biology from Cornell University. During this time, he encountered God through a campus Bible study and was baptized in 1990. He committed his life to Christ through the preaching of Rev. Moses Chow at the Chinese Mission Convention organized by AFC in 1992. He then spent the next two decades conducting biomedical research at several research institutes.

By God's grace, he served on the board of AFC from 2011 to 2015. Since 2015, Dr. Bor has served as the Executive Director of AFC. In 2022, he was inaugurated as AFC's third President, continuing to lead and further its mission: reaching Chinese intellectuals for Christ in this generation.

Foreword 3

LIFE TRANSFORMED, MISSION ACCOMPLISHED

Elder Elaine Kung

Ellen Yan's life embodies her steadfast faith in God, her unconditional love for her husband Bing and their children Reece and Mina, and her fervent passion to serve God's children and advance His Kingdom.

Reece, Mina, Ellen, Elaine, and Bing at AFC's 60th Anniversary in May 2023

Having Ellen and Bing in my *Called To Work* courses during COVID was a bright spot and a great blessing. We have become good friends and ministry partners over the past few years, visiting each other's homes in Massachusetts and California, celebrating AFC's 60th anniversary in Paradise, PA, with the entire Liang family, visiting the AFC founders' tombstones, and sharing in Ellen's joy as she prepared this manuscript and reflected on her memorable friendship with Mrs. Leona Choy.

I have had the privilege of witnessing God's sovereignty and mighty works in the Liang family in many up-close and personal ways, through one-on-one, one-on-two, and one-on-four sessions, staying in their home, serving at their church both in person and online, meeting their friends and students, touring their hometown, and visiting the children's college campuses. The list goes on and on.

Ellen and her family have accomplished the American dream to the utmost, but more importantly, they have also experienced the Kingdom dream in each of their personal lives. I am so encouraged by their family's harmony, unity, and togetherness in many areas of their lives —truly doing life together in their 7Fs: Faith, Fitness, Family, Firm, Finance, Fellowship, and Fun.

This book is another excellent example of how Ellen has lived out her desire to trust and obey God's calling for her to write this remarkable celebration of AFC's legacy, and to fulfill the dreams of the AFC founders through this compelling summary of their stories.

I can count the many blessings of how God has **transformed Ellen's life**, and how God has used her to **accomplish the mission** of telling the powerful AFC stories. We can experience the theme of D.I.V.I.N.E. intervention and orchestration throughout Ellen's writing journey and throughout this entire book. This acrostic represents some key reflections and recommendations for ***The Mosaic of the Divine Symphony — Legacy of Faith in the Land of Promise:***

Devoted to the Great Commission
Inspiring testimonies of trusting and obeying the Lord
Vigilant in creating lasting impacts on countless souls over decades
Instrumental in advancing God's Kingdom
Noble character displayed by the AFC leadership
Exalting Christ in all things for His glory

I am grateful for "growing up" with AFC since my college years in the 1980s, enjoying Rev. Moses Chow's inspiring messages in the US and in Hong Kong, admiring Rev. David Chow and Dr. Bor's servant leadership, and now serving on the AFC Board. Praise the Lord for Ellen's obedience and for the Liang family's dedication in making this book possible. This book promises to renew our passion for mission both locally and globally.

I pray that this book also stirs up a new generation of full-time missionaries at home, at work, in church, and in the community. May we all enjoy our work as we live out the Great Commission, serving Him as full-time Christians and missional disciples in every area of our lives. All Christians are missionaries. Rev. Billy Graham once said, "I believe one of the next great moves of God is going to be through believers in the workplace."

We can say that God is our CEO, based on Colossians 3:23: "Whatever you do, work at it with all your heart, as working for the Lord, not for human masters." As Christians, we are blessed to go to work with Jesus, instead of leaving Him at home or at church. We can say "Thank God It's Monday" and enjoy His **divine** intervention every day. We can keep an empty chair for Jesus at work, reminding us to partner with Him and engage in one-on-one conversations with Him for our work-related challenges, creative problem-solving, and conflict resolution.

Jesus is coming back soon, and we should feel the urgency to share the gospel wherever God has placed us — including in the workplace, where we spend most of our days. The workers are the largest mission force, reaching the largest mission field — the workplace — both locally and globally. Are you willing to play your instrument and join this divine symphony in fulfilling the Great Commission? Would you like to enjoy and pass on this legacy of faith in the Land of Promise? I encourage you to read this book with a new perspective, applying Ellen's faith journey to bless your own and to be a blessing to others. May your **life be transformed** as God uses you to **accomplish the mission** He has given you.

Elder Elaine Kung, born in Hong Kong, immigrated to Maryland as a teenager in 1980 and became a Christian in 1981. She received her B.S. from Cornell University and M.S. from Princeton University in Electrical Engineering and Materials Science Engineering. AT&T sponsored her Executive Education in the Business Schools of Columbia, Cornell, and the University of Pennsylvania's Wharton School. After 33 years of a rewarding career at AT&T, she retired—or reFired—from her Director role.

Elaine has been a passionate teacher, speaker, and coach for children, youths, and adults since 1986, sharing lessons from the Bible and her faith journey as a missional disciple at home, at work, at church, and in the community. She founded Called To Work in 1996 to encourage workers, equip leaders, and expand workplace ministry partnerships both locally and globally. During COVID, by God's grace, Elaine led the acceleration of the faith-at-work movement, mobilizing and multiplying missional disciples at work. At the 4th Lausanne Congress in Seoul, Korea in 2024, she launched the Global Day of Faith at Work (observed on May 1 each year), sponsored by Lausanne Movement Workplace Ministry and World Evangelical Alliance.

Her peak season included more than 20 one-on-one coaching sessions per month, giving 30+ talks each month, delivering 30+ series of courses and video programs that turned into more than 10 books. Among the 2,000 global students Elaine has taught since 2020, 50 have become trainers who, in turn, have used the Called To Work curricula to teach approximately 1,000 students in local and global communities.

Elaine serves on eight international boards, including Ambassadors for Christ, and chairs the Theology of Work Project Chinese Board. Elaine and her husband, Dominic, have been married since 1986 and are blessed with three generations.

PART ONE:

THE ENDURING LEGACIES OF AFC FOUNDERS

Chapter 1

THE REMARKABLE JOURNEY OF MOSES CHOW

A PRELUDE: WHISPER OF DESTINY

In the dim corridors of an ancient Buddhist monastery, where echoes of ages blend, a new father, wrestling with both joy and anxiety, sought insight from a monk known for his mystic foresight. "What future awaits my newborn son?" he asked, his voice trembling between hope and fear. A tense silence hung in the air, heavy with the promise of hidden truths, until the monk looked up, his gaze deep and knowing.

"Your son is entwined in a fate filled with shadows, marked by a chilling prophecy. Darkness will seek him out before he turns ten, as

My heartfelt thanks to Rev. David Chow, the eldest son of Rev. Moses Chow, for his generous photo contribution and invaluable feedback on the manuscript. This chapter draws primarily from Rev. Moses Chow's three autobiographies: *Let My People Go* (1995) and 骨肉之亲 (2007), *Let My People Go: Moses Chow 50 Year Missionary Journey* (2024), all published by Ambassadors for Christ, Inc., Paradise, PA malevolent forces keep a watchful eye," the monk said, his calm voice belying the serious warning it carried, chilling the father to the bone.

However, a ray of hope shone through the gloom. "If he can overcome these challenges and reach adulthood, he's destined for a life of great purpose." This glimmer of hope sparked a fragile optimism in the father.

Carrying this bittersweet revelation, he stepped back into the light, which now seemed to flicker uncertainly, reflecting the precarious path that lay ahead for his son. How would destiny shape his journey, a dance between fate and faith, for a child nestled in prophecy?

THE SPIRITUAL AWAKENING

Nestled within the vibrant landscapes of Shaoxing, Zhejiang province, mainland China, a child named Chupei Chow (周祖培) entered the world on November 9, 1925. His father, Peter Chow (周子卿), established a distinguished reputation in the world of business. Yet, his personal life was marked by the poignant loss of two wives to illness, a journey shadowed by grief yet lit by the hope of a family's warmth. This hope was rekindled with his marriage to Xiangde Zhao (赵向德), a young woman of 16, radiating with vitality, intelligence, and grace. Xiangde, whose lineage was graced by her father's eminent role within the fading echelons of the Qing dynasty's governance, brought a new dawn to Peter's life. Their marriage symbolized the melding of distinct yet harmonious spiritual traditions—Xiangde's roots in Buddhism and Peter's in Daoism.

The birth of Chupei Chow marked a turning point for Peter. Overwhelmed with joy, he sought the revelation of a Buddhist monk, questioning the future that awaited his long-awaited son. The monk's grave prophecy—that Chupei was marked by destiny for either an early demise or a significant future—cast a shadow over Peter's heart, prompting an almost overprotective love for the child.

Nurtured by the wisdom and affection of his father, Chupei set forth on a voyage of the mind, diving into the rich seas of classical Chinese literature under his father's tutelage. Through rigorous memorization exercises and the lighthearted moments spent on his father's back en route to school, Chupei was unknowingly preparing for the linguistic bridges he would later cross in a foreign land.

Yet, it was an invitation from a school friend that introduced Chupei to a world beyond the confines of his family's expectations. At a small Chinese Christian church, Chupei encountered the Holy Spirit in a profound and personal way, quietly accepted Jesus as his savior at the tender age of five!

A crisis soon beckoned at their doorstep, with Xiangde's health hanging by a thread. She was so gravely ill that despite Peter's every effort, he feared he might lose his third wife as her condition continued to worsen. In the midst of this despair, Chupei, inspired by his newfound faith, made a bold request: "Father, may the church pray for my mother?" Driven by desperation, Peter consented. Three devout women from the church entered their home, their prayers a chorus of faith that miraculously ushered in a tide of healing for Xiangde. After their prayers, Xiangde's condition improved—she was able to sleep, began to take food, and rapidly recovered. This miracle softened her heart, leading her to the church's welcoming embrace, though Peter remained aloof, his scholarly pride a barrier to belief.

THE CHOWS' JOURNEY TO THE NEW FAITH

During one reflective session, Chupei's Sunday school teacher planted a seed of courage within him, suggesting he share the gospel with his father. "But how can I possibly do that?" Chupei fretted, well aware of his father's skepticism toward God and the possibility of punishment should his insistence be perceived as annoyance.

"Take this Chinese Gospel of John home and give it to your parents," the teacher proposed. With a mixture of duty and apprehension,

Chupei placed the Gospel on his father's desk, a silent messenger of his newfound faith. Concealing himself as his father returned, Chupei watched anxiously through a sliver of space by the door.

"The Good News of John? Who is this John? What's this all about? Is this some foreign religious book? Get it out of my sight!" Peter exclaimed, his voice laced with suspicion, before dismissing the book with a flick of his hand.

Though disheartened by his father's initial rejection, Chupei didn't falter. He retrieved the Gospel and repositioned it on a different table, hoping for a change of heart. His persistence paid off when, driven by curiosity, Peter picked up the book once more. This time, something stirred within him as he read, "In the beginning was the Word (Tao), and the Word (Tao) was with God..."

"Interesting, it speaks of Taoism," Peter mused aloud, unknowingly echoing the divine orchestration that led him to this moment. The Holy Spirit worked quietly, softening his heart with every word he absorbed from the gospel. Chupei, scarcely breathing, observed his father engrossed in the Gospel of John, reading it from start to finish in a single session.

Upon finishing, Peter summoned Chupei with a newfound softness in his tone. "Where did this book come from?" he inquired. With a heart pounding against his chest, Chupei confessed his secret visits to the Chinese Christian church, bracing himself for the reaction.

"Take me there," Peter asked, prompting a mixture of relief and apprehension in Chupei as they made their way to the church. Behind those closed doors, conversations unfolded between Peter and the pastor, their contents unknown but undoubtedly profound, leaving Chupei in a state of hopeful anxiety.

This marked the beginning of a transformative journey for Peter, guided by the unexpected intersections of faith, culture, and divine intervention, with Chupei playing a pivotal role in bridging the worlds between his father and the gospel.

Over the ensuing months, Peter devoted himself to an earnest exploration of the Bible, his every moment consumed by the words and teachings contained within its pages. The Holy Spirit navigated through the intricacies of his Taoist beliefs and the barriers of long-held prejudices, illuminating a path of truth and understanding. At the culmination of this profound journey, Peter declared with unwavering conviction, "As for me and my house, we will serve the Lord (Joshua 24:15)." Xiangde, witnessing the transformation and spiritual awakening within her husband, embraced Christianity alongside him. Together with Chupei, they made a public affirmation of their faith, receiving baptism and stepping into a new life in Christ.

THE EXODUS

This decision meant confronting the deeply ingrained practice of ancestor worship, a cultural cornerstone that had been faithfully observed by their family. Recognizing the discord between this tradition and the teachings of their newfound faith, they faced a challenging crossroads. With courage and faith, they chose to forsake ancestral rituals in favor of a life aligned with Christian principles, marking a significant shift in their spiritual journey and familial legacy.

In 1931, a profound decree was set forth within the walls of Chupei's family home. His father, guided by a divine vision, instructed his wife to prepare a feast of unparalleled savor, destined for their ancestors, for one final time. These dishes were laid before the ancestral tablet in the grand Shrine of their ancestral hall, marking the end of an era.

Chupei, at the tender age of seven, was entrusted with a monumental task. Standing before the ancestral tablet, he bowed deeply and, mustering a voice far beyond his years, said, "This is the last meal you will receive from us. We bid you goodbye, for we are Christians now and can no longer worship you as before." This declaration marked a dramatic shift in the family's spiritual journey, echoing through the halls of their home.

Word of Peter's family's spiritual pivot swiftly permeated the clan, prompting a solemn assembly within the ancestral shrine. The Chows were a prominent family, their wealth rooted in expansive tracts of farmland that had sustained generations. Theirs was a life of communal harmony, where each season saw a different branch of the family orchestrating ancestral worship rituals, followed by the equitable distribution of farm profits—a tradition that ensured the prosperity and cohesion of the clan.

At the gathering, the air was thick with anticipation and the weight of tradition. Chupei's great uncle, a patriarch revered for his authority, steered the proceedings. Peter, Chupei's father, found himself at the center, the focus of many scrutinizing eyes. The men of the family, bearers of the clan's legacy, stood prominently, while the women, adhering to custom, observed quietly from behind a bamboo screen.

The confrontation was direct and charged with emotion. "It has come to our attention that you've embraced a foreign faith," the great uncle accused, his voice echoing off the ancient walls.

Peter, with a steadiness borne of conviction, replied, "Yes, it's true."

"And you intend to abandon the worship of our ancestors?" the elder pressed, seeking confirmation of what was, for many, an inconceivable breach of duty.

"Yes," Peter affirmed once more, his resolve unwavering under the weight of centuries-old tradition.

The elder's voice, laden with the gravity of the moment, continued, "Do you realize that in doing so, you relinquish all claims to inheritance and the benefits that come with it?"

"I am aware," Peter responded, his acceptance of the consequences signaling the depth of his faith.

Offered one final opportunity to recant, the question was posed, "Will you choose this Jesus over the veneration of our ancestors?"

Without hesitation, Peter declared, "I'd rather have Jesus."

The verdict was swift and irrevocable. Peter's family was to be excommunicated, stripped of their rights and possessions, and given mere days to vacate the home that had been theirs for generations. This edict marked the beginning of their exodus, a journey away from the life they had known into the uncertainty of faith.

Before their departure, Peter knelt before Chupei, placing his hands on his son in a gesture of solemn dedication. "Now, God," he prayed in a voice heavy with emotion, "I offer to you all that remains to me—my beloved son. From this day forward, I will call him Moses." His prayer was a fervent hope that his son, now named Moses, would be a beacon of faith, leading others from the darkness of sin to the light of salvation.

With heavy hearts but fortified by their faith, Moses and his parents left behind their ancestral home, setting out for Shanghai. There, in a humble dwelling shared with fellow believers, they continued their worship of the true God, their spirits undiminished by the trials they had faced.

THE CHALLENGING JOURNEY OF FAITH

In Shanghai, they discovered a renewed sense of mission. Peter transformed into a devoted servant of prayer, spending countless hours on his knees in supplication until his knees bore the calloused marks of his devotion, reminiscent of a camel's skin. With unwavering boldness, he took to the streets to share the gospel, his words imbued with a divine authority that allowed him to liberate those ensnared by malevolent spirits.

Peter earnestly sought to share the light of Christ with his elder brother, yet faced stern rejection, his brother's words cutting deeply: "Leave now. You are no longer my brother." Despite the pain of such rebuff, Peter's resolve remained unshaken; he continued to lift his family up in prayer, steadfast in his faith. In time, the seeds he planted through prayer began to flourish, leading to the gradual conversion of his family members to Christianity.

Moses' mother, too, was a pillar of faith, known for her fervent prayers. Instead of reprimanding Moses directly for his missteps, she guided him toward prayer, encouraging reflection and repentance through a gentle yet profound spiritual discipline.

Even as a young student, Moses displayed remarkable courage, sharing his faith with his peers. He embraced a transformation not just in belief but also in identity, changing his name from 周祖培, symbolizing ancestral cultivation, to 周主培, signifying cultivation by God.

The year 1933 marked a pivotal moment for eight-year-old Moses when he encountered Dr. Timothy Dzao (赵世光), a dynamic evangelical speaker, at a Sunday school convention. Dr. Dzao's message, imbued with spiritual fervor, deeply moved Moses, inspiring him to dedicate his life to God. This encounter not only marked a significant turning point in Moses' spiritual journey but also fostered a lifelong mentorship and friendship with Pastor Timothy Dzao, guiding him on his path of faith and service.

THE FIRST BRUSH WITH DEATH

At the tender age of nine, Moses was struck by a severe illness, suspected to be typhus. His condition quickly deteriorated, leading to a harrowing period where he exhibited all signs traditionally associated with death: absence of pulse, breath, and heartbeat. In line with Chinese customs during such times of loss, the family prepared for mourning by laying Moses's seemingly lifeless body on a door removed from its frame, as his father was away and unable to bear witness to these sorrowful proceedings. The anguish that enveloped Moses's mother and their relatives was palpable, a deep well of grief and disbelief.

The moment Moses pledged his future to God, his father's heart swelled with pride, yet his mother's spirits sank with worry. "I can't bear the thought of my bright boy limited to the life of a humble preacher," she lamented. "He's destined for greater, to thrive, not just survive. He should inherit the garment factory in Shanghai from his uncle, not wander in obscurity."

But the shadow of Moses's critical illness cast a pall over their dreams and aspirations. As Moses lay motionless, his mother's heart was torn with remorse and fear. Through her tears, she bargained with the heavens, "Oh Lord, if you spare him, I'll surrender my dreams for him. Let him follow Your path, even if it leads to the pulpit." Around her, the silence was heavy with skepticism, her late epiphany seemingly futile against the cruel finality of death.

Yet, in that moment of despair, the impossible unfolded. A sneeze erupted from Moses, jolting the room into stunned silence before erupting into incredulous joy. What was thought to be a young life lost was now a testament to the miraculous, as Moses stirred back to life as if awakened from a deep slumber, leaving all witnesses in awe of the divine power at play.

Overcome with relief and joy, his mother's faith was sealed with a fervent exclamation, "Son, now you belong altogether to God!" What had been a desperate plea was transformed into a solemn commitment, a celebration of divine intervention that underscored her unwavering belief in a God who listens and responds to the heartfelt pleas of His people.

THE SECOND BRUSH WITH DEATH

In the tumultuous year of 1937, as the skies over China darkened with the specter of Japanese warplanes, Moses's family sought refuge from the havoc, leaving behind the smoke-filled horizons of Shanghai for the relative peace of Ningbo. Yet, amidst this backdrop of upheaval, a different storm was brewing, one that would test the very fibers of Moses's spirit and body.

At age 12, right when life was supposed to be an endless stream of laughter, Moses faced a turn of events that seemed more like a plot twist out of a suspense novel than anything a kid should ever go through. It all kicked off with what was supposed to be a prank: one of his friends, in a moment of misguided humor, pushed him into deep, icy waters. Trouble was, Moses couldn't swim. Panic set in as the cold clutched at him, turning the laughter into shivers and setting off a chain reaction inside his body.

Before he knew it, Moses found himself battling an intense fever, one that doctors identified as malaria tropica. This fever clung to him like a shadow for ten long days. One night, feeling thirsty, he tried to get up for a drink but ended up collapsing on the floor, unconscious. The fever surged back fiercer than before. His condition was so critical, it was as if he were walking a tightrope between life and death.

In the heart of a storm-laden afternoon, where the heavens wept as if mourning, Dr. Ting, a beacon of compassion and a close confidant of Moses's father, took swift action upon hearing of Moses's dire condition. As the superintendent of a Christian hospital, he wielded his influence to secure Moses a place within its sanctified walls, a haven for those wrestling with the shadow of death.

Moses found himself in the grip of a peculiar trance, teetering on the edge of mortality. A surreal detachment enveloped him, as if his spirit had embarked on a journey, leaving the confines of his hospital bed behind. He wandered through a murky, rain-soaked street, his feet squelching in the mud, a lone figure akin to a boy scout with a backpack slung over his shoulder, venturing toward the unknown.

The world around him was deserted, except for the whispering rain and the somber echo of his footsteps. Drawn to the river's edge, he settled on a stone bench shrouded in fog, the river's opposite bank a hidden mystery beyond the veil. Darkness began to claim the day, a tangible sign of the uncertainty that lay ahead.

It was then that a stranger emerged, a figure from another time, clad in a raincoat woven from pine needles and a bamboo hat that seemed to dance with the wind. His words pierced the silence, "Hey, there's no more ferry boat service this afternoon. Go back!" It was a command, laden with an unseen urgency, compelling Moses to retreat from the precipice of the unknown.

As Moses's consciousness stirred, clawing its way back from the abyss, he awoke to the somber faces of doctors and the tear-stained cheeks of his parents in the intensive care unit, a sanctuary for those whose lives hung in the balance. The air was heavy with prayers and pleas to the Almighty, a testament to a family's unwavering faith. "Oh God, we have dedicated our only son to You, not once, but thrice, in body, spirit, and resolve. Why do You beckon him to Your kingdom now?" they lamented, their hearts laid bare before the Lord.

The miracle of Moses's return from the brink was nothing short of divine intervention, a moment of joyous reunion that rekindled hope and reaffirmed faith. In the aftermath of his ordeal, Moses felt a profound awakening within his soul, a certainty that his life was marked for a higher calling. Amidst the unseen battles, where forces of darkness sought to derail his destiny, Moses's resolve only strengthened, fueled by the undeniable sense of being chosen for a purpose far greater than himself.

This experience, this divine intercession, galvanized Moses's commitment to God's service, readying him for the trials and triumphs that lay on the path chosen for him by the Almighty. It was a testament to the living God, active not just in the hallowed stories of old but in the here and now, guiding, protecting, and calling His faithful to embrace their divine purpose amidst the tumult of life.

A PRAYER TO FULFILL OF THE GLOBAL MISSION

At age 13, Moses found himself captivated by the story of Hudson Taylor, the visionary behind the China Inland Mission. Full of curiosity, he questioned his father, "How come a foreigner felt called to venture into our nation and start a mission to share the gospel with people not from his own land? Why aren't we, the Chinese Christians, inspired to reach out beyond our borders in the same way?"

His father, reflecting on the question, responded with wisdom, "Son, let's entrust this aspiration to God, praying that He might empower you to embark on such a noble task—to carry the gospel across seas to those not of our own." Together, they knelt in prayer, with his father invoking blessings not only for Moses but for the generations to follow, asking that they might honor God with their deeds and dedication. This prayer, fervent and forward-looking, left a profound imprint on Moses's heart.

Years down the line, Moses would recount this pivotal moment to his children and grandchildren, illustrating how this prayer had been answered beyond measure. Indeed, God had steered Moses and his lineage toward the missionary path, broadening their ministry and faith to distant lands across continents, bringing countless souls to Christ.

THE LITTLE PREACHER

In 1943, amidst the echoes of a world in turmoil, Moses found his purpose within the walls of Bethel Bible School in Ningbo. It was here, under the guidance of an independent missionary, Mrs. Nickerson, a woman of Pentecostal heritage with unwavering faith, that Moses, alongside his friend Peter, delved into the depths of their beliefs. Together, they experienced the profound and life-altering baptism of the Holy Spirit, a moment that solidified their faith like never before.

Before even reaching the age of 16, Moses was entrusted with the sacred task of preaching. It was as if the divine hand itself guided his words, each sermon flowing with a power and conviction that belied his youthful appearance. His messages resonated so deeply with the hearts of those who heard him that he became known as "the little preacher," a title that spoke volumes of his spiritual maturity and eloquence.

Two years had woven their passage through time when an invitation, as unexpected as it was prestigious, found its way to Moses.

Endorsed by a Christian woman of devout faith, Moses was invited to a united annual Presbyterian conference as a special speaker. This marked a momentous first for him, stepping into the role of a conference speaker, a testament to his growing influence and divine calling.

Moses had been assured that someone would be there to greet him as he arrived by boat. Brimming with anticipation, he stepped off the boat, eyes scanning the crowd, but found no one waiting for him. Unfazed and fueled by faith, he made his way to the church alone. With every step, a quiet prayer echoed his footsteps, a reflection of his resilient spirit and the unseen guidance propelling him forward.

At the church's gate, he encountered only the doorkeeper, to whom he declared his purpose. "I've come for the conference," he stated, a simple proclamation met with a directive to wait. "The person in charge has gone to meet someone," the doorkeeper informed him, ushering Moses into a small deserted room, where time seemed to pause in solitude.

As the clock ticked away, the quiet was suddenly broken by the vibrant buzz of attendees, their chatter signaling the event's importance. It was then that Moses, the unassuming presence in their midst, caught the registrar's attention. "What's your name?" he inquired, a simple question poised to uncover an astonishing truth. "Chou[1] Chupei," Moses responded, his name floating through the air with an almost sacred resonance. "What? You're the one?" Disbelief washed over the registrar's face, his eyes darting up and down, struggling to reconcile the young man before him with the esteemed speaker he had envisioned. With a burst of realization, he dashed off, his voice elevating in excitement, "The preacher is already here!"

The initial murmur of disappointment that might have greeted Moses's youthful appearance dissolved as he took the pulpit. For in

1 The surname 周 is spelled as "Chou" in an older romanization system, while "Chow" is commonly used by families in the Chinese diaspora, adapted for easier pronunciation in English.

that sacred space, as he began to speak, the divine anointing upon his words transcended his age, weaving a sermon that captivated hearts and minds. By the sermon's end, the congregation was not just satisfied; they were elated, touched by a message that resonated with the profound joy and spiritual nourishment that only the blessed hand of God could provide. In this unexpected vessel, God's voice found its echo, reminding all present that in His kingdom, it is not the outward appearance that counts, but the readiness of the heart to be a conduit of His eternal wisdom and love.

THE DIVINE GUIDANCE

At the age of 18, Moses found himself navigating the turbulent waters of dating, his heart pulled in different directions by his affections for various young women. Seeking clarity amidst the confusion, he turned to God in prayer, hoping for a sign to guide his wayward heart. The answer came in an unexpected form during a voyage between Shanghai and Ningbo.

Aboard a steamship, Moses journeyed across the Suzhou River toward the sea. As the vessel transitioned between river and ocean, Moses's attention was captured by a solitary tree trunk bobbing aimlessly on the water's surface. This sight struck a chord within him, sparking a profound contemplation about destiny and divine will.

He contrasted the aimless drift of the tree trunk, subject to the whims of tide and time, with the purposeful voyage of the steamship. Unlike the log, which floated without direction or control, the ship, built from similar wood, was guided by a captain, charting a course with intention and destination. This distinction illuminated Moses's understanding of God's will versus the randomness of fate. Both the log and the ship faced the sea's challenges, yet their journeys and outcomes were markedly different.

This revelation became a metaphor for Moses's life and decisions. He realized that in surrendering to God's will, in boarding God's "ship" through faith, he embraced a life of direction and purpose, no longer adrift like the aimless wood but moving toward a divine destination. Emboldened by this spiritual epiphany, Moses wholeheartedly committed to following God's plan for his life.

Figure 1: Moses with his wife Wendy and daughter Grace in Shanghai in 1948.

On December 5, 1945, his journey led him to unite in marriage with Wendy Zee, a fellow believer whose dedication matched his own, ready to follow wherever God might lead. Together, they embarked on a life of faith and obedience, a testament to their trust in God's guidance. Their union was blessed with the birth of their daughter, Grace Chow, on April 12, 1948, in Shanghai, marking the beginning of a family legacy anchored in faith and commitment to God's will.

THE DIVINE CALLING

In the crisp winter of January 1946, Moses embarked on a transformative journey at the Eastern China Theological College in Hangzhou, a beacon of learning fueled by the Ling Liang Evangelical Association and the China Inland Mission. There, Moses honed his spiritual acumen, emerging not just educated but profoundly shaped by the experience. Before the ink

Figure 2: Moses with His Mentor Dr. Timothy Dzao.

on his diploma could dry in 1948, he was called to shepherd the Ling Liang Church in Shanghai, a testament to his exceptional training and divine calling.

As Moses adeptly navigated his dual roles, nurturing both his family and flock, a challenge arrived along with his spiritual guide, Dr. Timothy Dzao, a visionary with a heart for the globe. He just returned from the Dutch East Indies, his spirit heavy with the need for missionaries overseas. A church in Indonesia, once pastored by Dr. Dzao, was in dire need of a Chinese pastor, and Moses was his chosen candidate. Initially, Moses's heart was torn—his dedication to his current church, and his filial duties as an only son, all anchored him to China.

Despite the younger man's reservations, Dr. Dzao persisted, urging Moses to seek divine guidance. The church's deacon board gave their blessing, yet Moses faced the daunting task of convincing his parents. His father, though hesitant, offered his support, but it was his mother's plea that tested Moses's resolve: "Son, China also needs you. Many millions of people here need to hear you preach about Jesus. No, don't go. You are my only child. I love you more than my own life. Stay in China. I want you near me. I want to be with you all the time and listen to you preach. I would feel so desperate and lonely if you left." Then she continued, "Yes, I know I already dedicated your life to the Lord to serve Him, but you don't have to serve Him so far away."

Her words, laden with love and fear of separation, echoed the deep bond between them, her reluctance a stark reflection of her maternal love and the cultural expectations of filial piety. Moses felt helpless. "Mother, may we pray and leave the decision with God?" Moses asked. "Of course," she agreed, glancing at the motto on the wall: PRAYER CHANGES THINGS.

After days bathed in prayer, Moses's mother experienced a heart-changing revelation. Acknowledging the supremacy of God's will over her fears, she blessed Moses's mission, her words a poignant reminder of their eternal bond in God's grand design: "Son, though the difficulties and my objections are still there, I must obey God. You

Figure 3: Moses with his parents, his wife and daughter in 1948.

may go. My prayers go with you. If you are in the center of God's will, you are close to me. If you are far from the Lord, then you are far from me, too." Moses was very relieved when he got his mother's blessings.

In early March of 1949, Moses, alongside Wendy and their baby daughter Grace, barely eight months old, embarked on a journey away from Shanghai. Little did they know, their departure was divinely timed, a narrow escape from the shadows of persecution that would soon cloak Shanghai under Communist rule in May of 1949. This departure, unbeknownst to Moses, was a divine safeguard against the trials and tribulations that would ravage China, marking a poignant last goodbye to his father.

Throughout the turbulent decade of the Cultural Revolution (1966-1976) that engulfed China, the core members of Moses's family faced unprecedented trials. His father, steadfast in his faith until his last breath, was imprisoned, subjected to hard labor, and eventually died. His mother's relentless determination to stand by her son became a testament to her indomitable spirit. Amidst these daunting times, the unwavering resilience and faith of Moses's family glimmered as a lighthouse of steadfast devotion amidst the fiercest tempests of history.

For thirty years, an untraversable distance lay between Moses and his mother, a stark testament to the profound sacrifices demanded by a life of faith and the unpredictable path of answering God's call. Yet, across this expanse of time and separation, a deeper bond was nurtured, one rooted in prayer, faith, and an absolute trust in the ever-present guidance of God. This connection, invisible yet unbreakable, served as a source of hope, illuminating the path through life's trials and the ever-changing landscape of history.

THE FIRST FOREIGN MISSION FIELD—INDONESIA

As a Chinese-born missionary to venture abroad, Moses embarked on his mission field with a heart full of zeal but without the roadmap of experience to guide him. After ten days of sailing, he set foot in Jakarta, the sun blazing above him like a herald of the challenges to come. The unfamiliar faces and foreign tongues of Indonesia immediately enveloped him in a wave of homesickness, the distance from his homeland manifesting as a tangible ache in his heart.

Upon arrival, he and his family were warmly greeted by Pastor Zhengye Lin, a seasoned Chinese missionary, who ushered him to what would be his new spiritual home. However, on his very first night in Jakarta, Moses found himself at the center of an unexpected board meeting within the church, the topic of discussion being his living allowance. The question came direct and startling, "Pastor, how much money do you need?" Moses, taken aback by the forthrightness of the query, responded with humility, "I've just arrived and am still unfamiliar with the local situation. Surely, you all, being more acquainted with it, would know better than I."

In this new land, the hierarchy within the church was markedly different from what Moses was accustomed to. Here, the deacons held a stature above that of the pastor, effectively acting as the church's employers with the pastor as their employee. The church had seen a revolving door of pastors—seven in seven years—each unable to anchor the church amidst its financial storms. It was against this tumultuous backdrop that Rev. Dzao recommended Moses, hoping he would be the one to bring stability.

Moses addressed the board with a courage that belied his newcomer status, stating:

> Dear friends, my journey to Indonesia was directed by the Lord's hand, not by the pursuit of sustenance. My presence here isn't to seek comfort or to ensure my plate is always full. I'm here to serve, guided by a calling far greater than the need for daily bread. Let's make this discussion on finance the first and only of its kind. I'm here to fulfill God's work, even if it means receiving nothing in return. My commitment is to His will, and if He decides my path leads elsewhere, I'll follow, regardless of any material offer. The Lord is my true employer, my guidance and my provider. Thus, I suggest we keep our financial dealings as a matter between Him and me. I will look to the Lord for my needs and trust in Him alone to provide. He is my Shepherd, and in Him, I place all my trust and needs.

This bold stance set the tone for Moses's ministry, but it wasn't long before he faced another challenge. A few months into his mission, Pastor Lin, his initial guide and mentor in this foreign land, departed for other ministries, leaving Moses to navigate the complexities of his calling alone. This sudden shift thrust the full weight of the church's responsibilities onto Moses's shoulders, a daunting task for the young missionary far from home.

Language stood as Moses's first formidable challenge in Indonesia. Without prior exposure to the Indonesian language and lacking resources to learn it upon arrival, Moses was undeterred. He embarked on a rigorous self-taught journey, sacrificing sleep for study, dedicating his nights to language acquisition while shepherding his flock by day. In those quiet moments, he sought divine assistance, laying his linguistic hurdles at God's feet.

The heavens responded, endowing Moses with an extraordinary blend of linguistic aptitude, wisdom, and spiritual vigor. His relentless effort began to yield remarkable results. In just two years, Moses found himself preaching eloquently in Indonesian, his earlier missteps in language usage becoming fond anecdotes among his congregation, endearing him further to their hearts.

This genuine connection, fueled by his unwavering sincerity and spiritual depth, catalyzed the growth of his congregation from a modest gathering into a thriving community. From thirty to forty members, the numbers swelled to hundreds, peaking at five to six hundred devoted followers over seven years. Moses's journey from linguistic novice to beloved preacher stands as a testament to the power of faith, perseverance, and the transformative grace of God's gifts.

The lush tropical beauty of Indonesia, while breathtaking, brought with it a set of challenges for Moses and his family. The relentless heat, coupled with Moses's exhaustive ministry efforts, began to take a toll on his health. Night after night, the inability to find rest left him drenched in sweat, a testament to the physical demands of his calling. By the time Dr. Dzao visited him from Hong Kong in 1956, Moses was grappling with a significant decline in his health.

In the sweltering heat and humidity of the tropics, Wendy faced her own battles, as the demanding climate aggravated her arthritis. Amidst these personal challenges, the family of Moses saw rapid growth. They welcomed their first son, David Chow, into the world in 1949. Joyce, their second daughter, followed in 1951. The family continued to expand with the birth of their second son, Andrew, in 1953, and then their third son, John, in 1955. Managing a bustling household with five children ranging from infancy to primary school age proved to be a Herculean task for Wendy, leaving her both physically and emotionally exhausted.

Recognizing the toll this life was taking on Moses's family, Rev. Dr. Dzao stepped in with a lifeline, offering him a sabbatical to rest and further his studies abroad. Faced with a choice between Europe and the United States, Moses felt a divine nudge toward America, despite his longing for Switzerland.

Little did Moses know; this redirection was not merely a pause for rejuvenation but a divine intervention. The political landscape in Indonesia was on the brink of a seismic shift that would soon pose grave risks to Christians. Unbeknownst to him, his move to America would shield him and his family from the impending storm that would engulf Indonesia in 1965, a testament to the protective hand of God guiding them away from unseen dangers.

NAVIGATING INDONESIA'S COMPLEX RELIGIOUS LANDSCAPE

Previously under Dutch rule, Indonesia's landscape was dotted with descendants of Dutch settlers who introduced Christianity to the archipelago. However, the governmental reins were predominantly held by Muslims.

The Chinese community in Indonesia burgeoned through two significant waves of migration: the first between 1860-1890 and the second after 1920, following the relaxation of immigration restrictions by the Dutch. By the 1950s, of Indonesia's 138 million populace, 3.8 million were of Chinese descent, primarily practicing Buddhism, though there was a notable presence of Chinese Christians in need of pastoral care.

Amidst this diverse tapestry of faith and heritage, Moses dedicated himself to empowering local Christians, training them to spread the gospel across ethnic lines and beyond Indonesia's shores. In collaboration with Indonesian leader A. M. Tanbunna, Moses established the Missionary Training Institute in 1954. Moses further founded Gamaliel University, offering higher education to Chinese students in Jakarta in the same period of time.

However, tranquility was shattered on September 30, 1965, with a coup that spiraled into a dark period of mass violence and persecution, particularly targeting alleged communists. From October 1965 to March 1966, Indonesia was engulfed in one of its most harrowing chapters, with death tolls ranging from 80,000 to 1 million, including many Christians caught in the crossfire of religious tensions. The island of Buru became a grim detention center for around 10,000 people from 1969 to 1980, without the due process of a trial. Among those persecuted was Rev. Richard Lee, President of the Missionary Training Institute and a close ally of Moses, who endured years of imprisonment.

Figure 4: Moses with his family in 1955,

Yet, through these turbulent times, Moses was divinely safeguarded, destined to touch many lives for years to come. With the support of Rev. George Steed, a Missionary Director from OMF in Indonesia, as his guarantor, Moses found a new beginning in Allentown, Pennsylvania, where he joined Berean Bible School in the fall of 1956, marking the start of a new chapter filled with hope and continued service.

CONNECTING EAST AND WEST: UNITING THE WORLD

Upon setting foot in America by himself, Moses was met with challenges of colossal proportions, a stark contrast to anything he'd faced before. Grappling with the English language was his first hurdle; despite his linguistic prowess in Indonesian, English seemed like an insurmountable peak.

At age 31, Moses found himself in a sea of youthful faces, his seminary classmates mostly teenagers and young adults in their early twenties. The cultural chasm between his Chinese heritage and American ways was wider and deeper than he had ever experienced. Amidst this sea of youth, he stood out—not just for his age but also for his struggle with English.

An unexpected request to share his testimony in English at a gathering plunged him into a state of panic, reminiscent of a childhood incident where he nearly drowned. In that moment of desperation, Moses's plea to God soared in his native tongue, and miraculously, he found the words to express his faith. He spoke of the boundless love of Jesus, declaring, "Jesus is wonderful. To God, there is no division between east and west. We are all brothers and sisters, united in the vast family of Jesus Christ." The details of his speech faded from memory, but the essence of his message—a testament to unity and love—remained.

Despite these early trials, Moses threw himself into his studies with unwavering commitment, sacrificing sleep to absorb every lesson, even at the expense of his health. Yet, through it all, he felt the sustaining hand of God.

His presence in a local church soon became the subject of curiosity and amusement among many American Christians, for whom Moses was a living novelty, far removed from the caricatures of Chinese people they'd only seen in comic strips or in movies like those featuring the fictional character Charlie Chan.

An elderly gentleman's request to shake his hand, "You are the first one I ever saw," and the children's eager curiosity, touching him while exclaiming, "Gee, we never touched a Chinaman before!" revealed the deep-seated stereotypes and ignorance of the time. Unbeknownst to their innocent minds, their words echoed a derogatory term from a bygone era of Chinese laborers in America.

Through these interactions, Moses navigated the complexities of cultural misunderstanding with grace, embodying the spirit of unity he preached, and gradually, through his presence and testimony, began to bridge the gap between the two worlds.

THE DIVINE INTRODUCTION

In the heart of 1956, a memorable encounter unfolded as Mr. and Mrs. John Phillips, esteemed faculty members of Berean Bible School and missionaries with the Sudan Interior Mission, escorted Moses to the quaint town of Paradise, Pennsylvania. Their visit was to introduce Moses to a trio of remarkable individuals: Miss Christiana Tsai, and sisters Miss Mary Leaman and Miss Lucy Leaman.

Moses was already familiar with Christiana Tsai's inspiring tale from her widely acclaimed book, *Queen of the Dark Chamber,* which had reached global fame, was translated into 34 languages, including Braille, and was even adapted into a film. The prospect of meeting such a profound servant of the Lord filled Moses with great anticipation.

Seated beside Christiana's bed on a diminutive chair from Ming Deh Girls School in China, Moses found himself enveloped in the comforting darkness of her room. Engaging in heartfelt dialogue in their shared hometown dialect of Shanghai, a swift bond formed between them, rooted in their connections to Shanghai—Christiana's former home and Moses's pastorate.

This initial visit blossomed into frequent meetings, with Moses often finding solace in the "Room of Isaiah" on the second floor of their home. Their relationship deepened over shared prayers, meals, and conversations, echoing the warmth of family ties. To some, Christiana was akin to Moses's godmother, yet their mutual respect was always evident in their formal address—Moses as "Rev. Chow" and Christiana as "Miss Tsai."

Figure 5: Moses with Ted, Leona, and Christiana Tsai in 1956.

Their first meeting also coincided with the presence of Ted and Leona Choy, staff members of International Students, Inc., who ministered to international students at colleges and universities in the greater Philadelphia area.

This meeting marked the beginning of a relationship that none could foresee would profoundly alter their lives and significantly impact the spiritual journeys of innumerous others. Unseen divine orchestrations wove these encounters into the fabric of their destinies.

TRIUMPH THROUGH ADVERSITY

Upon completing his studies at Berean Bible School, Moses, ever seeking divine direction, pondered his next chapter. It was Rev. George Steed, Moses's steadfast ally in the US, who proposed Columbia Bible College (CBC) in South Carolina for advanced missionary training.

Emboldened by prayer and God's affirming nod, Moses embarked on the new journey to CBC in 1957, envisioning a future where he'd return to Indonesia, reuniting with his family and continuing his work at the Missionary Training Institute. Yet, the path God had in store for him began to unfold in unexpected ways.

Armed with just a smattering of English from a year at Berean Bible School, Moses embarked on the daunting journey through CBC's rigorous master's program. The challenge was Herculean. Eager to reunite with his family in Indonesia, Moses took on a full course load, aiming to accelerate his studies. However, the steep climb to academic excellence saw him placed on probation until he could secure a B+ average, alongside the monumental task of earning 30 credit hours and crafting a thesis.

His days were marathons, beginning before sunrise and ending well past midnight, a regimen that strained his health to its limits. As he neared the finish line of his studies, the physical toll manifested in rapid heartbeats and chest pains so severe, Moses feared a heart attack loomed on his horizon. Contemplating whether to halt his academic pursuit, he was eventually discharged from the hospital, the diagnosis not life-threatening but a clear signal his body demanded rest. Moses likened his CBC ordeal to "a cow being forced to climb a tree," a colorful expression capturing his uphill battle.

By his third year, the twin demons of physical burnout and financial strain nearly convinced him to quit. Health alarms and an empty wallet presented Moses with a gut-wrenching choice: part with the only piece of jewelry he had bought for Wendy to navigate through the financial storm.

During these challenging times, the Indonesian church stood as a steadfast beacon of support for Moses's family, their unwavering aid reaching across the miles. Despite this, Moses grappled with the sharp sting of separation, tormented by the fear that his children might slowly forget the face and love of their father.

Navigating the hardships, Moses unearthed a deep understanding of the struggles faced by international students in the US, especially those originally from Taiwan, Hong Kong, or Southeast Asia.

Defying the odds, bolstered by the encouragement of his professors and the solidarity of the Christian community, Moses emerged victorious from his trials, graduating from CBC as a shining example of God's miraculous provision.

THE DIVINE REALIGNMENT

Moses's deep longing to return to Indonesia and his cherished ministry was abruptly interrupted by a grave caution from his church staff. With Indonesia engulfed in civil turmoil and Christians facing severe threats from Muslim persecution, the land he wished to serve in had become fraught with perils. This new hurdle on his path underscored the unforeseen turns and the relentless unpredictability of walking in alignment with God's divine purpose.

Bolstered by the encouragement of Christiana Tsai and Ted and Leona Choy, Moses embarked on a journey with International Student Inc. (ISI), dedicating his efforts as a volunteer associate to the ministry among Chinese students in the US. The Choys, who had been integral to ISI's Chinese student ministry since 1955, welcomed Moses into a partnership that nurtured Bible study groups across various cities and states. Moses found a second family in Ted and Leona's home in Maryland and in the welcoming arms of Mary Leaman in scenic Paradise, PA.

In 1957, the trio orchestrated the inaugural Chinese Christian Student Summer Conference at Penn Grove Bible Conference Center. They invited esteemed Chinese Christian speakers to address students from campuses nationwide, sparking a tradition of annual gatherings that would endure for years. These conferences became pivotal moments for many attendees, including scholars, doctors, lay church workers, and pastors, marking the beginning of their spiritual journeys or deeper commitments to faith. Among them was a young Rev. Stephen Tong (唐崇荣) who, despite his tender age, graced the conference as a speaker and would go on to become one of the world's most revered evangelical pastors.

Moses's involvement in the Inter-Varsity Christian Fellowship Missionary Convention in Urbana, Illinois, in 1958 brought him face to face with a passionate wave of students responding to God's call, a significant number of whom were Chinese. This experience kindled a divine passion in Moses for these young individuals, navigating the unfamiliar waters of a foreign culture.

Through his engagement with Chinese students, Moses felt a profound connection to their journey—confronting academic and financial hurdles, overcoming cultural and language obstacles, enduring emotional isolation, and searching for spiritual fulfillment.

This critical phase honed Moses's mission to guide the Chinese international student community, setting the foundation for a ministry that would flourish, extending the gospel's reach to myriad Chinese students and scholars, illuminating their paths.

FROM RESISTANCE TO REDEMPTION: EMBRACING MINISTRY IN JAPAN

At the Pocono Mountains Christian Conference, Moses's path crossed with Mr. Norman Grubb from the Worldwide Evangelization

Crusade who, along with fervent prayers, encouraged Moses to consider a ministry in Japan. Rev. Dzao further impelled Moses to earnestly seek God's will for such a ministry.

Yet, the mere thought of serving in Japan was unbearable for Moses. Haunted by childhood memories of bullying by Japanese boys, witnessing unfathomable atrocities in Shanghai, Nanking, and his hometown Ningbo during the war, and hearing tales of relentless cruelty throughout Indonesia and Southeast Asia, his heart was heavy with anguish. "Oh no, Lord, anywhere but Japan!" was his desperate plea to God as he struggled with the idea of ministering to people associated with so much personal and historical pain.

Despite his reservations, God's guidance was unwavering, nudging Moses toward Japan. Reluctantly, Moses envisioned ministering only to the Chinese community there, hoping to steer clear of any direct engagement with the Japanese.

Yet, God charted a different course. When Moses arrived in Yokohama, he was met with an unexpected gathering of a thousand Japanese, and was faced with the challenge of preaching about love—a lesson in stark contrast to his personal misgivings toward them. Through the guidance of John 3:16, he found solace in the teaching that God's love is unbounded, even embracing those whom he, Moses, could scarcely bear in thought. It was a divine moment, shaping him into a voice for the very ministry of grace he had wrestled with, seamlessly weaving the threads of redemption and compassion for the Japanese and Chinese alike.

His first sermon in Japan was the beginning of a transformative journey of faith, drawing countless people to embrace Christ. This was a powerful proof that God's purpose is not only to heal but to wholly renew and bridge hearts across divides with the open-hearted message of the gospel, transforming sorrow into a unity of spirit.

By 1959, Moses took on the role of pastor at the Tokyo Overseas Chinese Church, and he prayed intensively for his family's safety amidst the turmoil in Indonesia. Miraculously, in 1960, after four years of separation, Wendy and their five children were reunited with Moses in Japan, spared from the devastating violence that would later engulf Indonesia in 1965.

Yet, the transition to Japanese society posed its own set of challenges for Moses's family. Adjusting to a new language, culture, and schooling system was daunting, particularly in a society where the Chinese were not warmly received.

Through it all, Moses remained committed to his calling in Japan, serving with unwavering faith until yet another unexpected turn of events in 1962 left him astounded, a testament to the unpredictable journey of following God's lead.

THE CALL TO AMERICA: THE 3RD MISSION FIELD

The vibrant student ministry led by Ted and Leona Choy was flourishing. In a pioneering move in 1958, they established the Chinese Christian Church of Greater Washington, D.C. After much deliberation and prayer for divine direction, Ted and Leona reached out to Moses with a heartfelt request, inviting him to shepherd this newly birthed congregation as its first pastor in 1962.

While Moses was still contemplating this significant call, an unexpected twist occurred—a phone call from the Vice Consul revealed that his family's visa to the US had been miraculously approved. The news bewildered Moses; he hadn't filed any application. It soon came to light that the initiative had been taken by the Chinese Christian Church in the US, which had applied on behalf of Moses and his family.

Upon sharing this providential development with his Tokyo Overseas Chinese Church family, where he served as pastor, Moses braced for their reaction. To his astonishment, the congregation's response was one of sacrificial support. Despite their desire for him to continue his ministry with them, they recognized a greater calling for Moses in America. They saw an urgent need for someone to minister to Chinese students in the US, many of whom were losing their spiritual moorings away from home.

With hearts united in this vision, the Tokyo Overseas Chinese Church did something extraordinary. They committed to funding Moses's journey to America, offering not just their blessings but tangible support to ensure Moses and his family could embark on this new missionary endeavor. "We are willing to pay for you and to send you from Japan to the mission field in America," they declared, showcasing a remarkable example of global Christian fellowship.

Thus, Moses found himself on the cusp of yet another missionary journey, this time being sent from one foreign land to another, with the mission to reach out to Chinese students across the vast expanse of the United States.

THE BIRTH OF AFC

Guided by divine confirmation from multiple sources, Moses wholeheartedly embraced the call to lead. In 1962, he relocated with his family to Washington, D.C., moving into the second house of Ted and Leona's twin house on 16th Street Northwest. There, he took the helm of the burgeoning Chinese Christian Church of Washington, D.C., which had been founded by Ted and Leona four years earlier and rapidly expanded under his stewardship.

Starting with modest gatherings in Ted's living room in 1958, the church's meeting place moved to Moses's living room in 1962, then to his remodeled basement, and eventually to larger spaces to accommodate the growing congregation. Ultimately, the church built a new building on Piney Branch

Figure 6: Moses's Family in 1963.

Road, which later added an educational building.

Figure 7: AFC Board Members in late 1970s.

In a spirit of collaboration and after thoughtful prayer and strategic planning, Moses, alongside Ted and Leona, founded AFC. The nonprofit Christian organization was officially inaugurated in Washington, D.C., on May 6, 1963. The AFC's first headquarters were in Ted and Leona's living and dining rooms, after the first Chinese church they founded moved next door. Upstairs were their living quarters, where they provided hospitality for traveling Chinese students. This marked the beginning of a pivotal chapter in their ministry, addressing the spiritual needs of Chinese students and communities across the United States.

Moses and Ted took on the roles of co-directors at AFC, with Moses also fulfilling his pastoral duties at the Chinese church. Their complementary strengths propelled AFC's mission forward. Leona's invaluable assistance in managing office operations and extending warm hospitality to all who came AFC's way greatly contributed to their success.

Balancing his responsibilities as pastor and co-director, Moses dedicated himself to both roles with remarkable zeal, often working from dawn till midnight with scant time for himself. It was through sheer grace that he navigated this demanding dual ministry, his tireless efforts a testament to his deep commitment to serving God and nurturing the faith of the Chinese Christian community in America.

A DIVINE GIFT TO AFC

In 1966, inspired by a divine calling, Christiana Tsai and the Leaman sisters decided to gift their picturesque farm in Paradise,

Pennsylvania, to AFC. This generous act was rooted in their shared vision with Moses, Ted, and Leona Choy, whom they first encountered in 1956. United by a fervent desire to share the gospel with Chinese students and intellectuals, they envisioned their land as fertile ground for spiritual growth, outreach, and training the next generation of student leaders.

Seeing the potential to further their mission, AFC gratefully accepted the Leaman property, committing to transform this serene farmland into a beacon of hope and a hub for spiritual education and evangelism. The vision was clear: reaching Chinese intellectuals for Christ in this generation in order to reach the world.

As the years unfolded, the ministries under AFC and the church blossomed, necessitating dedicated leadership. After earnest prayer, Moses made the pivotal decision in 1969 to step down from his pastoral role, dedicating his full energy to the mission of AFC.

In 1972, a momentous event unfolded as President Richard Nixon of the United States embarked on a historic journey to the mainland of China. This visit was not merely a diplomatic mission; it was a beacon of hope, piercing through the dense fog of the Cold War, signaling the beginning of a thaw between two mighty nations. The icy silence that had long lingered between the United States and China was finally broken, heralding a new era of dialogue and understanding.

By grace, in 1979, the seeds sown by President Nixon's visit bloomed into full diplomatic relations between the two countries. The barriers that had once seemed insurmountable were now crossed, and the once-impenetrable bamboo curtain of China was lifted, not by the hands of man alone but by the guiding hand of the Almighty.

Thus, Chinese students from mainland China began to make their way to American campuses. What began as a mere trickle soon transformed into a mighty torrent, as if the floodgates of exchange had been flung wide open. Yet, this was no surprise to the Divine Architect; for God, in His infinite wisdom, had already prepared His servants of AFC and other mission organizations for such a time as this. Many

Chinese Christians had long prayed for China to be open to the gospel, affirming in faith, "It is not if China opens, but when."

Guided by a divine call, these faithful stewards found themselves at the beginning of an extraordinary movement of hearts. With open arms and hearts filled with faith, hope, and love, they were ready to plant the gospel's seeds in the hearts of students who had traveled far from home. In this beautiful journey of life, every detail is woven by the Master Craftsman, revealing again that across the sweep of time, God is tirelessly at work, steering history and unveiling His grand design.

In 1974, a dream woven from the unity and foresight of many took form with the establishment of AFC's new headquarters, a vision brought to life through the Leaman sisters' boundless generosity. This key transition from the bustling life of Washington D.C. to the tranquil haven of Paradise, PA, echoed the harmonious chord that was struck a century before when Rev. Charlie Leaman embraced his mission to China in 1874. It marked AFC's spirited rise to prominence as a cornerstone of the Chinese Christian organization in North America.

HOMEWARD BOUND: THE JOURNEY TO HOMETOWN

In 1978, after 15 years of devoted service with AFC, Moses took a sabbatical and became a pastor at Hong Kong's Bread of Life Church. In 1979, by God's merciful hand, Moses was able to return to his ancestral land, Ningbo—a place he had longed to see since his departure in 1949.

Invited by the Chinese government and the Three-Self Church as part of a delegation of overseas Chinese pastors, Moses felt the weight of his divine calling. At a crucial meeting with government authorities responsible for religious policy, Moses was asked if he had any suggestions or requests.

Figure 8: Moses with his mother and his wife in 1978.

With bold faith, Moses made three significant requests to the Chinese authorities: the reopening of churches so Christians could have places to gather, the reopening of seminaries to train pastors, and the release of Pastor Ming Dao Wang, who had been imprisoned for 22 years.

Miraculously, all three requests were granted. Later, many churches and seminaries reopened, and Pastor Ming Dao Wang was released from prison on January 9, 1980. God's Spirit was evident during that trip, as Moses baptized people in their bathtubs during his trip.

Separated for 30 years, Moses's reunion with his mother was deeply emotional. They had not been able to communicate directly in all that time, not even through letters, as correspondence from overseas could have endangered her. Moses always dreamed of reuniting with his mother while she was still alive, especially since his father had perished during the Cultural Revolution, leaving behind a legacy of love and loss.

His mother was overwhelmed, scarcely believing it wasn't a dream, having often imagined reuniting with her only son, whom she had reluctantly sent on a missionary trip in early 1949. Who could have imagined that this departure would lead to a 30-year separation? After their reunion, Moses brought his mother to the United States, where she lived with his family until she was called to the Lord in 1993.

ANSWERING THE CALL: MISSIONS BEYOND BORDERS

Summoned to venture into lands beyond the familiar embrace of his homeland, Moses heeded the divine call—Zambia, Thailand, Vietnam, and Kazakhstan awaited his arrival. With a shepherd's heart, he was drawn thrice to the bustling city of Hong Kong where, with gentle hands, he tended to the spirits of those under his care. Celebrated for the depth and passion of his sermons, Moses became a conduit through which the Holy Spirit reached and transformed lives around the world. His very presence stood as a luminous beacon of hope, a remarkable sign of God's guiding hand, paving the path for him as a distinguished Chinese missionary, a unique instrument in the grand symphony of the Lord's divine plan.

CHINESE MISSION CONVENTION: THE BEACON OF EMPOWERMENT

After his sabbatical, Rev. Moses Chow returned to AFC in 1981 as AFC President. Together with newly recruited Director of Literature and Chief Editor of *Ambassador* magazine, Edwin Su, and his son David Chow, who had been with AFC since 1976 and was now the Executive Director, Moses spearheaded the launch of the first triannual Chinese Mission Convention (CMC) in 1983. Despite numerous challenges, the convention was a resounding success.

By God's grace, 300 attendees gathered, meeting the requirements of the rented venue. Rev. Moses served as one of the main speakers. The theme, "A New Force in God's Kingdom," sought to ignite a missional vision among Chinese students and inspire Chinese churches and Christians to engage in missions. This convention laid a strong foundation for future CMC gatherings.

Since its inception, the Chinese Mission Convention (CMC) has been held every three years, and later every year rotating between California, Texas, and the East Coast, and drawing over 35,000 participants in total. It has become a crucial platform for rallying Chinese Christians around evangelism, both locally and globally. Over 7,000 individuals have heeded God's call to missionary service, leaving indelible marks across the globe through their unwavering commitment.

A LIFE OF UNWAVERING DEDICATION UNTIL RESTING IN GOD'S ARMS

After the first CMC convention in 1983, Moses was invited to serve as a retreat speaker in Dallas, Texas. When Dallas Chinese Fellowship Church was established in Dallas, Moses was invited to be their pastor. Despite his ongoing role as President of AFC, he felt a clear calling to serve in Texas. In 1985, he moved his family, now consisting of his wife and mother, to Dallas. There, he successfully balanced his duties as both the church pastor and the leader of AFC's student ministry in Texas.

In 1986, Moses was diagnosed with a serious heart condition. Despite doctors recommending immediate surgery, Rev. Moses was determined to deliver his speech at the 2nd Chinese Mission Convention in Washington, D.C. With two doctors seated in the front row, closely monitoring him and fearing a heart attack at any moment, he courageously delivered his message. By God's grace, Rev. Moses completed his speech successfully. In January 1987, he underwent quadruple cardiovascular bypass surgery in Dallas. He was hospitalized for nine days, followed by two days in a coma, and then another nine days during which he could neither eat nor sleep due to the impact of medication.

By God's grace, Rev. Moses gradually regained his health. After a long period of recuperation, he formally retired from AFC, concluding 25 years of dedicated service.

However, Rev. Moses continued his devoted service even after retirement. In 1989, he was invited to return to Hong Kong to pastor the Hong Kong Bread of Life Church for the second time. In 1992, he was called again to pastor the Dallas Chinese Fellowship Church. By 2000, he was once again invited to lead the Hong Kong Bread of Life Church (Lin Liang Church) for the third time, a role he held until 2002, when a stroke severely deteriorated his health, prompting his return to the US for recuperation.

His dedication to the Lord remained unwavering until his passing on October 13, 2008, at the age of 83.

A LEGACY OF FAITH: THE JOURNEY AND GLOBAL IMPACT OF AFC

Rev. David Chow became President of AFC in 2012, carrying forward his father's legacy with unwavering dedication. His fervent devotion to God's work, especially within the Chinese community, testified to the enduring faith and commitment that defined his lineage.

Under the guidance of strong leaders, AFC continued to flourish, establishing the family ministry, single's ministry, and the AFC bookstore. In 1985, the Mainland Chinese Ministry Department was created. AFC further advanced with the unveiling of the modern Great Commission Training Center in 2013, a 13,600-square-foot, state-of-the-art facility equipped to host up to 250 attendees, becoming a central hub for training events. The thriving Chinese Christian Faculty Network, single's conferences, and retreats have enriched countless lives. AFC also established campus ministries in major cities across the US.

By 2021, the ministry had expanded its reach through a comprehensive bookstore and distribution center with resources in traditional and simplified Chinese, dispatching over 5 million pieces of literature across North America and more than 33 countries. Approximately 52 campus ministers and associate ministers serve AFC on nearly 48 campuses in North America, Europe, and East Asia. In 2024, AFC entered a new chapter, transitioning from its long-standing bi-monthly Christian magazine in Chinese, which had faithfully reached 20,000 subscribers, to a modern digital format. Now, the *Ambassadors Audio Magazine* is delivered weekly, offering uplifting and inspiring content that continues to bring hope and encouragement to its audience.

Rev. David Chow officially retired in November 2022 after 46 years of dedicated service. His successor, Dr. Yeou-Cherng Bor, committed himself to the ministry under Rev. Moses Chow's preaching at CMC in 1992. Dr. Bor graduated with a Ph.D. from Cornell University and spent 16 years as a dedicated scientist in biomedical research at the University of Virginia. Since 2015, he has served as Executive Director. In 2021, he was named President-elect and on May 14, 2022, he was inaugurated as the third President of AFC, continuing to carry forward the organization's mission.

A HERITAGE OF DEVOTION: THE CHOW FAMILY'S LEGACY OF FAITH AND SERVICE

Rooted in Peter Chow's fervent prayers, a legacy of devotion to the Lord was born. His desire for his descendants to serve the Lord has blossomed through generations. The Chow family embraced this calling wholeheartedly, and the commitment continued to flourish, with many of his grandchildren also dedicating their lives to serving

Figure 9: The Chow Family reunion in 1994.

the Lord. This enduring commitment showcases the power of prayers to shape the path of many, generation after generation.

Rev. Moses Chow's journey was a beacon of divine purpose, leading numerous Chinese individuals to God's kingdom. This legacy, intertwined with AFC's mission, stands as a tribute to lives immersed in faith, service, and cultural integration. Through ongoing evangelism and community enrichment, AFC perpetuates this vision, drawing individuals closer to God and nurturing a legacy of spiritual leadership and cohesion. AFC's impactful endeavors reveal the dynamic ways God operates through His servants, manifesting His love and truth among His people.

Chapter 2

TED AND LEONA'S CROSS-CULTURAL CRUSADE FOR CHRIST

PRELUDE: LOST AND FOUND

In the early nineteenth century, within the bustling coastal city of Swatow, now known as Shantou, a tale of devotion unfolds. A young man, burdened with worry for his blind, missing mother, embarks on a relentless quest. Friends and relatives join in the search with shared fervor, yet the city keeps its secret well hidden.

As days blend into restless nights, hope dwindles until, at last, in the forgotten silence of an abandoned house, the young man's heart finds its solace. There lies his mother, enveloped in shadows, choosing

I want to extend my gratitude to Mr. Richard Choy, the elder son of Rev. Ted and Leona Choy, for his invaluable feedback on the manuscript. This chapter draws primarily from Rev. Ted Choy's autobiography, *My Dreams and Visions*, Mrs. Leona Choy's autobiographies, *Czeching My Roots* and *Slow Boat to China*, as well as *Curtain Call*, all published by Golden Morning Publishing, Winchester, VA.

solitude over the warmth of home, ready to embrace the end. What drove her to this lonely precipice? What secrets lie in the depths of her choice? This is not merely a story of a son's search for his mother but a journey into the heart of faith, hope, and divine mystery.

Come, let us journey together through tales woven with the invisible threads of God's handiwork, manifest in ways beyond our comprehension, assuring us that in the depths of our despair, solitude is a stranger. Let the narrative of a son and his sightless mother illuminate our path, leading us to a profound revelation and the might of a living God actively shaping our existence.

FAITH ACROSS GENERATIONS: THE CHOY FAMILY'S SPIRITUAL ODYSSEY

In the early nineteenth century in Swatow, medical solace was scarce. Only the healing hands of missionary doctors, whose clinics dotted the landscape like beacons of hope, provided treatment for the sick.

In this era of simple means and complex beliefs, a young entrepreneur, gripped by excruciating stomach pains, found himself at the threshold of one such beacon. Desperation knitted tightly with pain, he made a solemn vow to the missionary doctor who tended to him: if he were to be healed, he would open his heart to the Christian faith. It was a promise made in the shadow of agony, yet destined to kindle a light that would forever alter the course of his life.

Healed by the compassionate care and fervent prayers of the missionary, the young man, true to his word, embraced Jesus Christ as his Savior. His newfound faith was not a quiet ember but a blazing fire that he could not, would not, keep to himself. As a respected businessman, his vocal allegiance to this "foreign religion" drew eyes and ears, stirring the air of Swatow with whispers of change.

Yet, this story of faith was not without its trials. The young man's widowed mother, a devout idol worshipper, was engulfed by a tempest of anger upon discovering her son's conversion. So deep ran her devotion to the old ways that she chose exile over acceptance, hunger over harmony, fleeing the family home to wage a silent protest against her son's faith.

The entrepreneur, bound by love and duty, embarked on a fervent search for his mother. His heart was heavy with a dread that only a son's love could know—the fear of losing his mother not just to blindness caused by her life's toil but to a chasm of beliefs that seemed insurmountable.

When he found her, frail and refusing food in an abandoned dwelling, he did not despair. Instead, he lifted her in arms strengthened by faith and carried her home. Prayer and hope became his refuge and, with a heart full of love and a spirit undeterred, he implored God to bridge the vast expanse between belief and disbelief.

The power of persistent prayer, the gentle persuasion of Christian friends, and the relentless dedication of a missionary teacher who visited their home gradually illuminated the mother's heart. In what can only be described as a miracle, she not only embraced Christ as her Savior but also renounced her idols, becoming a beacon of faith in her own right.

Her mornings were dedicated to prayer, her voice rising in the early light, a testament to her devotion. She would open her door and pray loudly at her front door publicly. She prayed for her family, present and future, laying a foundation of faith that would outlast her earthly sight. Blind in body but clear in spirit, she became the matriarch of a legacy that flourished in faith, generation after generation. The woman's name was Yang Hiang-sui (楊氏).

Figure 10: Ted Choy's parents.

This young man, Hang-nguan Chua (蔡漢源), along with his wife Kweng-huang Chan, later emerged as a pillar of the Christian community in Hong Kong. Not only was he one of the eight founders for the Swatow Christian Church in Hong Kong back in 1923, but he also carved his name in the annals of commerce as a distinguished Christian entrepreneur, founding the Swatow Drawn Works Co. His life was a testament to faith in action, blessed with a bustling household of ten children. Among them was his fourth son, Ted Choy, who carried forward the blazing torch of their spiritual legacy.

Ted Choy, inheriting the rich spiritual heritage of his family, harbored an unwavering passion for Christ that burned brightly within him. This fervor was not content to remain a flickering flame; it sought to ignite hearts across continents. In 1963, Ted and his wife Leona, along with Rev. Moses Chow, founded AFC, an organization that stands today as one of the most influential Chinese Christian organizations in North America.

FROM CHINA TO THE US: TED CHOY'S SPIRITUAL VOYAGE

Ted Choy (蔡锡惠) was born in 1916 in Swatow, where he spent a childhood wrapped in joy and curiosity. At the tender age of 12, he was sent to Hong Kong, embarking on a new chapter of his life filled with education and discovery. It was here, amidst the bustling streets and new experiences, that Ted's love for music found a home in a church choir. His time at La Salle College was transformative, marking the moment he embraced Christ as his personal Savior and stepped into a life of sincere faith.

In the heart of the 1930s, the renowned evangelist Dr. John Sung, a man celebrated for his academic excellence in chemistry from Ohio State University, felt a divine call to serve the Chinese people. In a symbolic act of total surrender to God's calling, he cast his worldly achievements into the sea as he journeyed back to China. Dr. Sung, with his fervent spirit and unyielding dedication, became an iconic figure, inspiring countless souls across China and Southeast Asia with the simple yet profound message of the gospel. Ted, witnessing Dr. Sung's impassioned commitment, felt a deep stir within his heart. Moved by Dr. Sung's dedication, Ted pledged his life to God's service during a revival conference, marking the beginning of his unwavering journey in faith.

After completing high school, Ted pursued his theological studies in Nanjing, eager to deepen his understanding of divine truths. However, the tumult of the Sino-Japanese war led him to continue his education at the Canton Bible Institute in Hong Kong, where he graduated in 1939. Amidst his peers, Ted stood out with his aspirations, yearning to further equip himself for ministry by seeking higher education in America.

With barely $100 in his pocket, Ted crossed the vast ocean to attend the Evangelical Free Church Seminary in Chicago, now known as Trinity Evangelical Divinity School. The school welcomed him warmly, waiving his tuition fees and embracing him as a testament to their missionary endeavors. Ted's years at the seminary were filled with humility and hard work, from shoveling snow to tending the school's heating system, each task performed with the dedication of someone preparing for a lifetime of service to God. This journey of faith and determination paints the portrait of a man wholly devoted to his calling, narrative rich with warmth and inspiration, highlighting Ted's profound journey from a joy-filled childhood to a life consecrated to serving the divine.

Upon completing his seminary education, Ted faced a world embroiled in the turmoil of the Sino-Japanese war. Heeding the advice of his family, who feared for his safety amidst the conflict, Ted chose to remain in the United States, embarking on further theological studies at Wheaton College in Wheaton, Illinois. The cost of attendance at Wheaton was steep, challenging Ted to balance his studies with various jobs to secure his daily needs.

It was during these trying times that Ted witnessed the unwavering faithfulness of God. Miraculously, whenever a significant financial deadline loomed, Ted would discover an anonymous envelope in his post office box, containing the exact sum he required. This series of divine interventions affirmed the Lord's promise to provide for those He calls into His service.

Amidst the academic rigor and divine encounters at Wheaton College, Ted's heart was drawn to a young woman named Leona Spryncl. Leona, with her own unique story as the daughter of first-generation immigrants from Czechoslovakia, captivated Ted's affection. Their paths crossed in this place of learning and spiritual growth, weaving together their lives in a tapestry of love and shared commitment to faith. This period at Wheaton was not just a time of academic advancement for Ted, but a season of profound personal growth and the blossoming of a love that would enrich his journey of serving God.

HERITAGE AND HOPE: LEONA'S SPIRITUAL JOURNEY FROM CZECHOSLOVAKIAN ROOTS TO WHEATON COLLEGE

Leona's roots trace back to Cedar Rapids, Iowa, where she was born in 1925 into a family of Czechoslovakian immigrants. Her parents, Frantisek Spryncl and Marie Rompotlova Spryncl, proprietors of a bustling local eatery, found their days consumed by the demands of their business. This led Leona to spend her formative years under the watchful eye of her live-in paternal grandmother, Frantiska Plachy Spryncl, affectionately known as "Baba."

Figure 11: Leona's grandmother.

Leona was Baba's shadow, trailing behind her, sometimes peeking out from the sanctuary of Baba's ample apron whenever shyness took hold. It was in Baba's lap that Leona discovered the world of Bible stories and hymns, all delivered in the Czech language, Baba's mother

Figure 12: Leona's parents.

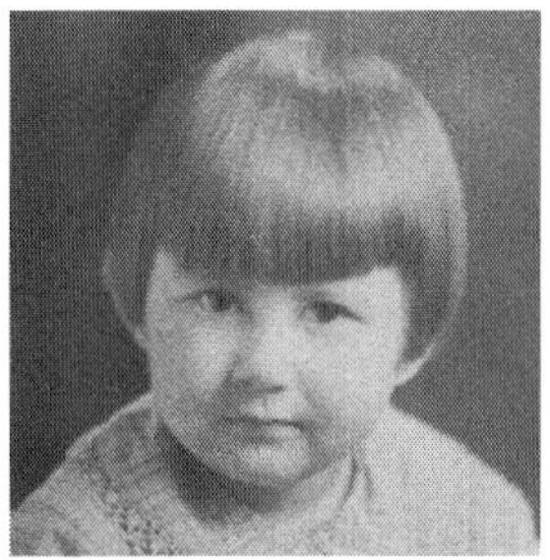

Figure 13: Young Leona

Figure 14: Leona (age 14) with her parents.

tongue. These moments with Baba, steeped in faith and tradition, became Leona's treasure trove of childhood memories. Baba's unwavering commitment to her faith, evidenced by her ever-present, well-thumbed Czech Bible and her heartfelt prayers, left an indelible mark on Leona. It was from Baba that Leona learned of an ancestor who was martyred for his faith in Moravia, highlighting the dual legacy of religious persecution and poverty that propelled her family to seek a new life in the United States in 1907.

Raised in the embrace of a Czech church, Leona ventured into an English-speaking congregation at the age of 12. In that transformative period, Leona cultivated an intimate relationship with God, deeply moved by the Holy Spirit's power. She was asked an important question: "What is the purpose of man?" She found her answer in the assertion that man's ultimate purpose is to glorify God and enjoy His presence. Inspired by a profound statement from one of Andrew Murray's works, "God is ready to assume full responsibility for the life wholly yielded to Him," Leona set forth on her journey, anchoring her life in this powerful conviction.

The vibrant faith she encountered there moved her so deeply that, by 16, she had dedicated her life to God. Inspired by the lives of Christian luminaries like Andrew Murray, D.L. Moody, and Hudson Taylor, Leona aspired to join their ranks as a renowned Christian author.

Upon graduating from high school, Leona's journey led her to Wheaton College, the very institution she had dreamed of attending. It was there that her path crossed with her future husband, marking the beginning of a shared life spanning 45 years, devoted to service in God's name.

THE DIVINE MATCHMAKING

On the inaugural day of an anthropology course at Wheaton College, where Leona had registered, Professor Alexander Grigolia introduced a unique twist: he declared that students would keep the same seats they chose on that first day for the entire semester. Amidst this, Leona strolled in fashionably late, only to find the class already a mosaic of occupied chairs. With a dramatic flourish, Professor Grigolia pointed her to the spotlight, "You, the girl back there, come up front and sit in this empty seat for the rest of the semester." And just like that, she found herself next to Ted Choy, in a plot twist none could have scripted.

Ted and Leona struck up an acquaintance with remarkable ease, and it wasn't long before Ted, charmed by Leona's presence, invited her out. Initially, Leona hesitated, seeing Ted more as a friend than a romantic interest, despite his earnest declaration that they were destined to marry—a conviction he believed was divinely inspired. Leona, with a hint of amusement, countered that she had received no such divine memo.

Despite her reservations, Ted's unwavering persistence gradually won over Leona, and she agreed to a few outings together. However, their budding romance was not without its challenges. The year was 1944, a time when societal norms frowned upon interracial relationships, placing Leona in a precarious position within her social circles. Meanwhile, the world outside was embroiled in the throes of the Sino-Japanese War, a conflict that compelled Ted to make a bold decision. He resolved to join the Marine Corps, a move that startled Leona with its suddenness and gravity. "If I were to be injured or worse, not return, you'd regret it," he half-joked, though the weight of his words hung in the air. Just a semester shy of completing his degree, Ted enlisted, soon finding himself on his way to Tianjin, China, as a specialist interpreter with the First Marine Division, leaving behind a budding relationship and an uncertain future.

During Ted's two years in China, his letters to Leona, sent almost daily, formed a steadfast link that kept their connection alive. The military's offer of free postage was a small consolation in his loneliness. When Ted walked back through the gates of Wheaton College, donning the proud uniform of a Marine, he had already captured Leona's heart. His letters, filled with thoughts and dreams, showcased the depth of his character, his clear vision for the future, his unwavering integrity, and his relentless perseverance.

Figure 15: Ted in the US Marine Corps

Ted and Leona sought guidance from two pivotal figures in their journey: Dr. V. Raymond Edman, the college president, and Professor Alexander Grigolia, the head of the Anthropology Department who almost divinely assigned their seats on the first day of class. With blessings received from both, they felt encouraged and ready to take the next step—sharing their news with their parents.

Navigating this relationship proved challenging for both sets of parents. Before Ted departed Hong Kong for America in 1939, his father's parting advice was clear: "Make sure you don't marry an American girl!" To which Ted responded, "Don't worry, father, that's not in my plans."

Leona's parents faced an even steeper challenge. Having never encountered a Chinese person, their only reference was a caricature from old tales—a laundryman with a pigtail living down by the railroad tracks. Imagine their surprise when they met Ted: a suave, tall figure dressed sharply in a business suit, his words gentle, carrying a subtle British accent. This offered them a moment of solace. Yet, as the sole guardians of their only daughter, accepting her choice to marry someone from a culture so alien to them, and then watch her move across the world for missionary work, was a bitter pill to swallow. The thought of possibly never seeing Leona again weighed heavily on their hearts. Learning of her engagement and imminent plans to set off for Hong Kong before tying the knot left them reeling, struggling to grasp the rapid changes unfolding before them.

Figure 16: Ted and Leona in 1947.

Leona, with her cum laude honors, graduated in May, and Ted graduated in August, setting the stage for their marriage.

Blessed by divine favor, Ted was warmly accepted into their family, culminating in a majestic wedding within their Czech church on the incredibly hot day of August 23, 1947. Iowa's heat, peaking at 102 degrees without the comfort of air conditioning, caused the candles to wilt in their stands. Under her veil, Leona felt the day's intensity, her face marked by sweat and the heat seeping through her beautiful white Chinese silk wedding dress, a heartfelt gift from Ted's parents.

VOYAGE OF VOWS: LOVE AND FAITH ACROSS THE PACIFIC

Three months after their vows, Ted and Leona, radiant with love, journeyed to California to board the venerable yet unrefined vessel, the USS General M.C. Meigs, setting course for Hong Kong. Men and women were quartered separately, with both Ted and Leona assigned to top bunks near the heating pipes, only reuniting at meals. Ted and

Leona's nights were spent in the embrace of the ship's gentle sways, their dreams entwined despite the distance. Their daily reunions at mealtime became fleeting oases of companionship in the vast sea, their love a beacon through the storm's fury.

Navigating the ocean's capricious temperament, their month-long voyage was marked by challenges from turbulent waters to mutual seasickness. Yet, these hardships only fortified their connection, showcasing their resilience and deepening their unity. As 1948 dawned, they arrived in Hong Kong's harbor, greeted by the eager anticipation of over a hundred well-wishers—Ted's family, friends, and allies, all there to welcome them and introduce Leona to her new chapter. Amid these joyful reunions, Leona was unaware that her farewell to her parents would be her last with her father, who passed away unexpectedly at 59 while she was abroad.

FAITH AND FAMILY: THE CHOY LEGACY IN HONG KONG

In Kowloon, Hong Kong, Ted embraced his calling as the pastor of the Swatow Christian Church, a role he fulfilled with devotion. Within the span of three years, their family blossomed with the arrival of three sons—Richard, Clifford, and Gary—bringing joy and a whirlwind of activity into their lives. Amidst this bustling domesticity, Leona found herself immersed in the duties of motherhood, her days rich with the challenges and delights of raising their children, even with the support of a household helper. Yet, in the moments she could carve out, Leona dedicated herself to teaching Christian education to fellow educators and contributing her leadership to child evangelism meetings, her contributions a testament to her unwavering commitment to her faith and community.

Originally, their hearts were set on spreading their faith among the people of the mainland. However, the shifting sands of geography and politics at the time rendered this dream unattainable. With the rise of the Chinese Communist Party around 1949, missionaries once stationed across the mainland found themselves compelled to leave, altering the course of their mission in profound ways.

A JOURNEY OF FAITH AND DUTY: THE CHOY'S SINGAPORE SOJOURN

In 1952, Ted received an invitation to lecture at the Singapore Theological College. The young family, with their trio of children—the eldest a curious toddler of three and the youngest a tender infant of three months—set sail for the vibrant city-state of Singapore. It was a journey marked by hope and the promise of new beginnings.

However, just as they were settling into this new chapter of their lives, a sudden storm struck back home. Only three months into their stay in Singapore, a somber message traveled across the seas: Leona's father had unexpectedly passed away. The grief was compounded by the news that Leona's mother, now a widow, was battling illness and required constant care. The family stood at a crossroads, their hearts heavy with the weight of their next decision.

Driven by love and a sense of duty, Leona made the heartfelt decision to return to the United States. She braced herself for the challenging month-long sea voyage ahead, now as the sole protector of her young children. It was a departure tinged with both sorrow and resolve, leaving Ted behind, tethered to his teaching duties in Singapore.

The journey home was nothing short of a trial, navigating the high seas with two toddlers and an infant. Yet, it was a testament to the resilience and faith of Leona who, by grace, safely guided her family into New York harbor on Thanksgiving Day 1952. Transitioning from the warmth of Singapore to the brisk chill of the US winter, the family faced further challenges. The cold season brought with it illnesses that taxed Leona further, especially as she cared for her ailing mother. In this time of need, the support of Leona's aunt, who came to stay and assist the family, was a beacon of hope and strength, illustrating the power of family bonds and divine grace in the face of adversity.

FAITH WITHOUT BORDERS: THE MINISTRY AMONG INTERNATIONAL STUDENTS

Upon concluding his teaching endeavors in Singapore, Ted returned to reunite with his family on American soil, fueled by aspirations to establish his roots and expand his ministry within the US. At the cusp of this new venture, he faced the pivotal challenge of obtaining US citizenship. In the midst of this slow-moving process, Ted remained undeterred. He embraced the opportunity to enrich his spiritual insight, enrolling in a master's program in Religion at the University of Iowa. Within the hallowed halls of this academic sanctuary, Ted embarked on a profound journey into the realm of divine truths, his heart and intellect in harmony, eagerly awaiting the day he could wholeheartedly call the United States his home.

This intellectual and spiritual quest was a transformative period, during which Ted became acutely aware of the spiritual needs of international students, a realization that would shape the course of his future endeavors.

Graduating with a newfound depth of knowledge, Ted and Leona turned their attention to a cause close to their hearts—the vibrant community of international students navigating life on American campuses. Their path led them to International Students, Inc., where they dedicated themselves to supporting Chinese students who had crossed oceans in pursuit of education. With most of these students arriving from the diverse cultures of Southeast Asia—none from mainland China due to stringent government restrictions—their ministry filled a crucial gap.

Driven by a profound vision to forge connections and elevate spirits, they served Chinese students from 1955 to 1962. Their journey led them to Philadelphia in 1955. By divine arrangement, in 1956, they visited Mary Leaman and Christiana Tsai on the same day that Moses Chow arrived from Berean Bible School. What seemed like a coincidence was, in fact, orchestrated by the divine hands of God. This serendipitous encounter transformed them into lifelong partners, united by a shared vision and passion: helping Chinese international students.

Figure 17: The Choy's family in 1963.

Recognizing the vision and need, Dr. Robert Finley, president of I.S.I., invited Ted to establish the Chinese Student Department at the organization's Washington, D.C. headquarters. Thus, in 1957, Ted and Leona moved to Washington, D.C., where their mission flourished. There, Ted's passion took him on a journey across the United States, from coast to coast, fostering communities of faith and fellowship through Chinese Bible study groups on college campuses. Their work not only nurtured spiritual growth but also crafted a tapestry of shared experiences, bridging cultures and hearts in the academic world. Moses Chow, an international student himself, joined as a volunteer associate of I.S.I., further strengthening their efforts.

In 1957, Ted and Leona, with the support of Moses Chow, launched the inaugural Chinese Christian Student Summer Conference at Pinebrook Bible Conference Center. Esteemed Chinese Christian speakers gathered to inspire students from campuses nationwide. This event ignited an annual tradition, becoming a significant milestone for many attendees and marking the beginning of a lasting legacy.

The momentum from this conference inspired the creation of *Ambassador* magazine, a publication that sought to weave a tapestry of spiritual support across US campuses. With Ted overseeing the printing and distribution, the magazine emerged as a vital resource, offering guidance and connection to Chinese students navigating their faith journeys far from home. This endeavor not only fortified the existing Bible study groups but also fostered a sense of community among Chinese students across the nation, echoing the profound impact of their collective ministry.

In 1958, they established the Chinese Christian Church of Greater Washington, D.C. The ministry quickly flourished, and in 1962, after much prayer and seeking God's guidance, they extended a heartfelt invitation to Rev. Moses Chow, who was then serving as a pastor at the Tokyo Overseas Chinese Church in Japan, to become their inaugural pastor. They even took the initiative to apply for US visas for his family on his behalf.

With God's invisible hand at work, the Tokyo Overseas Chinese Church supported Rev. Moses Chow's journey to the US, sending him as their own missionary. They even raised funds to cover his family's travel expenses.

To accommodate Rev. Moses Chow, his wife, and their five children, Ted and Leona purchased the house next door to their own. Rev. Chow moved his entire family across the ocean to serve as the church's inaugural pastor. This moment marked a significant milestone in their spiritual journey, reflecting God's guiding hand in their mission.

A LEGACY OF LAND AND LOVE: THE BIRTH OF AFC

In the year 1963, a trio of kindred spirits—Ted, Leona, and Moses Chow—were united by a divine vision to ignite a beacon of faith across North America. Thus, Ambassadors for Christ (AFC) was conceived, destined to become a vanguard in nourishing and empowering the faith of Chinese Americans. This marked a pivotal chapter in their spiritual odyssey, with both Rev. Ted Choy and Rev. Moses Chow serving as co-directors.

By 1966, through divine inspiration and fervent prayer, Mary A. Leaman, Lucy A. Leaman, and Christina Tsai performed an act of profound generosity, bequeathing 110 acres of lush land to AFC. This land, consecrated by their faith and vision, laid the cornerstone for a sanctuary destined for spiritual growth and the forging of communal bonds.

With Ted, Leona, and Moses Chow at the helm, AFC flourished into a stronghold of faith for the Chinese American community, a symbol of divine grace and a force for transformative change. The influence of AFC transcended its initial dreams, weaving a profound tapestry of faith that touched countless souls across the continent.

Figure 18: Ted and Leona in AFC

In 1974, a new chapter began with the dedication of AFC's headquarters, marking a significant move from Washington, D.C. to the historic Leaman property in Paradise, PA. This event occurred exactly a century after Rev. Charles Leaman departed from this very land to embark on his missionary journey to China in 1874, where he eventually passed away.

As it is written in John 12:24, "Very truly I tell you, unless a kernel of wheat falls to the ground and dies, it remains only a single seed. But if it dies, it produces many seeds." Similarly, Psalm 145:4 reminds us, "One generation commends your works to another; they tell of your mighty acts." The enduring spirit of Rev. Leaman's faith continues to inspire and flourish through the generations, encouraging Chinese intellectuals to reach out to their fellow countrymen.

Ted devoted 18 years of his life to AFC, serving with unwavering dedication until his retirement in 1981 at the age of 65. During his tenure, he witnessed AFC's remarkable evolution from a fledgling campus ministry into a nationwide beacon for the Chinese Christian community. With grace and a profound sense of fulfillment, he passed the torch to the next generation of leaders.

A COVENANT OF FAITH: THE ENDURING POWER OF ANCESTRAL PRAYERS

In the year 1979, as the world watched President Nixon extend the hand of diplomacy to China, a door long shut by the "bamboo curtain" creaked open, permitting a trickle of eager visitors to pass through its threshold. Among these pioneers were Ted and Leona, who embarked on a journey to Shantou, Ted's ancestral home, guided by whispers of the past and the gentle hand of Providence. Their quest bore fruit in the rediscovery of Ted's grandmother, a tale recounted with reverence in our opening narrative, "Lost and Found." Nestled in a place where time seemed to pause, they found her resting place, untouched by the ravages of the Cultural Revolution. It stood solitary, not amidst a sea of stones but alone, bearing witness to the ages. The towering headstone, inscribed with the name "Yang Hiang-sui, Mother and Grandmother of the Choy family, 1846-1929," remained unscathed, a testament to her legacy. This sacred site had been spared, legend held, not only for its secluded location beyond the village bounds but also due to a tale that whispered a curse upon those who dared disturb her peace, bringing illness and death upon their households.

Figure 19: Ted at his grandmother's burial site in 1979.

The air around Ted and Leona seemed to thicken with sanctity as they approached the grave. It was as though they stood on holy ground, the veil between the temporal and eternal thinned by their presence. Ted, with a heart swelling with reverence, recalled the divine lineage bestowed upon the Choy family through his grandmother's faith. Together, they prayed, their voices joining in a sacred plea that the seeds of faith sown by his grandmother would blossom across generations. They envisioned a future where their descendants would embrace the Christian faith, a lineage unbroken until the gathering of saints at the coming of Christ. Their prayers, whispered into the ether, were a covenant for their family's salvation and God's unwavering guardianship throughout their earthly journey.

Ted and Leona were profoundly moved, their souls stirred by the palpable presence of a spiritual heritage that spanned generations. The prayers of Ted's blind grandmother, it seemed, had traversed time, a beacon guiding her descendants through the tumults of life. Leona, too, felt the enduring embrace of her own grandmother Baba's prayers, a testament to the unbreakable bond of faith and family. In this sacred moment, Ted and Leona were not merely visitors to a grave; they were pilgrims at the altar of their ancestors' faith, witnessing the enduring legacy of prayers that echo into eternity.

PILGRIMAGES OF FAITH: EMBARKING ON SACRED MISSIONS TO CHINA

After his retirement, driven by a profound aspiration to offer solace and encouragement to the beleaguered Christians of China, Ted initiated an independent ministry known as the "English Tutoring Center (ETC)." Alongside Leona, he made many heartfelt pilgrimages to China, each journey laden with Bibles, training materials, and cassettes. Their mission was not just to teach English but to forge deep, personal connections, serving as Christ's ambassadors to those hungry for knowledge and faith.

Upon his retirement, Ted's adventures to China became a sacred mission, illuminating the lives of many with the gospel's radiant hope. With Leona by his side, they navigated this noble path together, embodying the spirit of missionary zeal.

With a heart attuned to the gentle whisper of compassion, they meticulously shepherded numerous souls from the United States to the heart of China. Leona visited China fourteen times, each visit a testament to her unwavering commitment to serve with kindness and to weave together the lives of those she met with the threads of divine grace.

The couple was blessed with the opportunity to visit numerous house churches, witnessing firsthand the indomitable spirit of Chinese Christians. In the face of relentless persecution and adversity, without the aid of foreign missionaries, the Christian faith flourished in secrecy, growing in numbers and strength far beyond anyone's wildest imaginations.

Ted and Leona bore witness to the Holy Spirit's miraculous work within China, demonstrating the power of faith to transcend boundaries and endure through the darkest of times. Leona, with a writer's touch, encapsulated their experiences in two poignant volumes, Touching China and Slow Boat to China. From 1979 to 1989, their devotion to the Chinese people burned brightly, a fervent zeal that only concluded when Ted was called to his heavenly home on November 9, 1992, at the age of 76.

THE MIRACLE OF FAITH: LEONA'S DIVINE AWAKENING

In the year 1974, amidst the bustling labor for the Kingdom, Leona found herself at the heart of a divine orchestration. Tasked with the monumental endeavor of erecting the new headquarters for AFC in the serene lands of Paradise, Pennsylvania, and orchestrating the monumental transition from Washington D.C., her days were consumed by sacred service. Yet, it was during this season of fervent activity, at a routine health examination, that a tempest brewed—a diagnosis of cancer, veiling her spirit in shadows of dismay. Words faltered to encapsulate the tempest within her soul, and in her distress, she lifted her voice to the heavens, seeking solace in the divine during her crucible of introspection.

It was then that the Holy Spirit, as gentle as the morning dew and as profound as the deepest seas, enveloped her being. Through a celestial embrace, the Spirit unveiled the essence of her toil—that her endeavors, though noble, were powered by the strength of her flesh rather than the boundless currents of the Holy Spirit. Like a chariot yearning for flight without the grace of wings, Leona recognized her efforts as akin to navigating the path of righteousness bereft of the Divine's empowering instruments. Her labor was an offering of zeal, yet it was detached from the very source of life, akin to a vessel striving against the tides without the guidance of the stars.

In her moment of revelation, Leona surrendered her entirety to the Almighty, immersing herself in the divine presence that transcends understanding. Baptized anew in the Holy Spirit, she was cradled back into an intimate communion with the Creator. Compelled by a deep longing for restoration, she found refuge in a Presbyterian church that regularly offered healing services. Embraced by prayers and anointed with oils, she returned home enveloped in tranquility.

Dawn broke with the promise of her final examination before the looming shadow of surgery. Yet, in a testament to divine intervention, physicians stood in bewildered awe as the malady that once cast a dark veil over her future had vanished, like mist before the rising sun. No longer bound to the surgeon's table, Leona wept tears of joy and gratitude, her heart a chalice overflowing with praises to the Most High.

This crucible of faith realigned the compass of her soul, revealing a divine order: God's presence as her foremost pursuit, her family as her cherished garden, and her service in the Kingdom as a joyous expression of love. She awakened to the sublime truth that dwelling in Him, nurtured by the ceaseless flow of the Holy Spirit, is akin to branches flourishing on the Vine—bearing fruit not by toil, but through the effortless grace of the One who sustains all.

Thus, from the ashes of physical tribulation, Leona emerged, her eyes unveiled to the wonders of the Spirit. With a heart ignited by heavenly fire, she embarked on a pilgrimage of discovery, traversing the expanse of the nation. From sanctuaries to stadiums, from halls of learning to gatherings of the faithful, she sought the wisdom of shepherds and delved into the depths of sacred texts. Her quest culminated in the creation of Powerlines, a book that distilled the essence of her journey and the revelations bestowed upon her—a beacon for all who seek to understand the gifts of the Holy Spirit and to walk in the unceasing flow of divine power.

HEAVENWARD JOURNEY: CELEBRATING A LIFE OF DIVINE SERVICE

In the silent wake of widowhood that gently enveloped her life over three decades past, Leona embraced her divine vocation with a heart reignited. With the shadows of loss casting long behind her, she devoted herself with unwavering zeal to the ministry of the written word. Alongside her eldest, Richard, she laid down the cornerstone of Golden Morning Publishing, assuming the mantle of Executive Director—a role she adorned with unparalleled grace for more than 25 years.

Figure 20: Leona at age 96.

Her path serendipitously wove through the ether when her son Richard, a craftsman of faith and innovation, birthed WTRM-FM, tenderly known as the Southern Light

Gospel Music Network. For 30 years, under Leona's prescient stewardship as Board President, the station flourished, navigating through eras of expansion and renewal. Moreover, her voice, for a span of five years, became a lighthouse through her daily radio broadcast, emanating hope and enlightenment to countless souls.

Leona was a truly remarkable writer, whose talent and compassion left an indelible mark on many lives. She played a pivotal role in bringing to life Christiana Tsai's second book, Christiana Tsai. Her skilled pen also graced the pages of Ted Choy's autobiography, My Dreams and Visions, and she faithfully assisted Rev. Moses Chow in writing his life story, Let My People Go. Beyond these, Leona was the authorized biographer of Andrew Murray, capturing his essence for posterity.

Leona's warm and kind personality shines vividly in Christiana Tsai's second book. When Mary Leaman fell critically ill and needed urgent hospital care, Christiana Tsai turned to their most trusted friend, Leona Choy, who lived 125 miles away in Silver Spring, Maryland. Leona arrived at record speed and drove them to the hospital emergency room. Without Leona's assistance, the arduous journey to the hospital seemed impossible. Christiana could not bear to be separated from China Mary, yet her own medical condition made it difficult for her to endure the fast speed of the ambulance.

Leona's involvement in helping Christiana Tsai write her book fostered a deep and intimate bond between them. Since Christiana spent all her time in a dark room, most of the writing and revisions had to be read to her countless times. Through these moments, Leona's compassionate spirit and unwavering dedication not only brought Christiana's words to life but also solidified their cherished friendship.

Leona's legacy is profoundly etched in the annals of literature. As an author, editor, collaborator, and writing coach, she brought forth over 55 books, her words bridging cultures with translations in numerous languages. Through her literary tapestry, she has woven threads of faith, wisdom, and transformation, touching hearts far and wide.

Figure 21: The Choy family at Leona's memorial service on March 13, 2023.

On March 2, 2023, Leona shed her earthly suit to be cradled in the arms of the Lord at the age of 97. In celebration of a life resplendently lived as Christ's emissary, her family and friends gathered, their spirits buoyed by the fulfillment of a prayer shared between Ted and his cherished grandmother. The Lord's answering whisper echoed through the continuation of their legacy, with generations of their lineage steadfast in the service of the Divine.

PART TWO:

THE LEAMAN LEGACY

GUARDIANS AND BENEFACTORS OF AFC LANDS

Chapter 3

THE LEAMAN FAMILY HERITAGE & CHARLES AND LUCY LEAMAN

EXODUS FROM SWITZERLAND

In the shadow of the seventeenth-century turmoil, Europe was scarred by the Thirty Years' War, leaving devastation in its wake. Switzerland, like many nations, bore the brunt of this conflict. Amidst the chaos, the Mennonites faced relentless persecution, their faith

I am deeply grateful to Dr. Ivan Leaman for his graciousness in reviewing and correcting my manuscript multiple times. This chapter draws heavily from his insightful article: Leaman, Ivan B. "The Remarkable Leaman Family of Leaman Place." Mennonite Life. Pennsylvania Mennonite Heritage, January 2017.
The primary sources of information about Rev. Charles Leaman and Mrs. Lucy Leaman in China were drawn from Presbyterian Church in the U.S.A. (Old School). "Annual Report of the Board of Foreign Missions of the Presbyterian Church, in the United States of America. 1871-1921." HathiTrust. Accessed September 29, 2022.
The sources for this chapter also include the following books:
Tsai, Christiana. *Queen of the Dark Chamber: The Story of Christiana Tsai.* Paradise, PA: Ambassadors for Christ Inc., 1986
Collins, Donald L. *The Admiral's Guard.* Tucson, AZ: Old Pueblo Publishing LLC, 2013.
Choy, Leona. *Curtain Call from the Dark Chamber.* Winchester, VA: Golden Morning Publishing, 2018.

making them targets. Among these courageous souls was Peter Leman (the family surname was changed to Leaman later), born around 1670 in the serene valleys of Bern. Raised in an Anabaptist family, Peter's early years were marked by displacement and hardship. Seeking refuge, he moved to Germany, where he married and started a family with five children.

Driven by dreams of a better life, Peter embarked on a journey to England and then across the Atlantic. In August 1717, after the passing of his wife, he and his children—Peter, Christian, Jacob, Barbara, and Mary—arrived in Philadelphia after a perilous month at sea. They were part of a larger tapestry of persecuted believers seeking sanctuary in the New World, much like the Mayflower pilgrims of 1620.

IN THE LAND OF PROMISE: THE LEAMAN FAMILY LINEAGE

In 1681, King Charles II awarded William Penn a vast expanse of land in America, which Penn named Pennsylvania. An English Quaker, Penn envisioned this new territory as a sanctuary for persecuted Christians across Europe, dubbing it the "Land of Promise." Guided by his Quaker principles, Penn established a government that embraced religious tolerance, democracy, and individual freedoms. This vision of a haven drew many Swiss-German Mennonites between 1710 and 1756, with a significant number finding new beginnings in Lancaster County.

Figure 22: The gravestone of Peter Leman

Among these settlers was Peter Leman, who arrived in 1717 and secured 300 acres of land. A diligent farmer, Peter expanded his holdings to 700 acres by 1735. He married Ann, and together they had six children, adding to his five from a previous marriage. Peter's success in land development ensured a prosperous future for the Leman lineage.

Peter Leman (1670-1741) left a rich legacy. His land was divided among his sons, with John Leman (1721-1759) inheriting 300 acres and Isaac Leman (1725-1776) and Daniel Leman (1727-1783) the remaining 400 acres. Today, the memory of Peter and John Leman endures at the Mellinger Mennonite Cemetery.

Peter's descendants dispersed into various denominations. His son John remained on the homestead, helping to establish the Lampeter Mennonite Meetinghouse, later known as the Mellinger Mennonite Church. Among John's descendants, Dr. Ivan Leaman continues to uphold the family's spiritual heritage and legacy.

Peter's youngest son, Daniel Leman, fathered 16 children. Daniel's son, Christian Leman (1763-1846), inherited half of his father's estate in Lampeter Twp. and raised six children there. furthering the thriving Leman family tradition. After Christian left the ancestral land and moved some miles east to Leacock Twp., he continued the family legacy in Leaman Place. His branch joined the Leacock Presbyterian Church, where their cemetery stands as a testament to their enduring faith

THE RISE OF LEAMAN PLACE

In 1794, the construction of the Lancaster-Philadelphia Turnpike transformed travel, passing through Paradise, PA, where the Reynolds family had established a substantial stone inn. Christian Leman, sensing opportunity, sold his Lampeter lands in 1795 and relocated to Paradise. In 1802, he acquired the Reynolds farm and inn, making it the Leaman family homestead.

Henry Leaman (1799-1887) inherited his father's business acumen and, by 1827, expanded the family holdings by purchasing an adjacent 36-acre property. In 1834, he built a three-story hotel alongside the

Figure 23: Leaman Place railroad and the hotel.

Philadelphia-Columbia Railroad, which spurred the development of a small village. This burgeoning community, soon known as Leaman Place, featured a dozen homes, a telegraph office, and a school.

Henry Leaman and his wife Catherine Amanda had eight children: Mary, William, Henry, John, Frank, Edwin, Charles, and Rosh. Four of their sons achieved remarkable success: William became a distinguished lawyer; Henry (1839-1923) and Rosh became esteemed doctors; and Charles (1845-1920) pursued missionary work in China. Charles's story is a pivotal exploration in this book, highlighting his significant role as a missionary and his dedication to carrying on the family legacy.

Among the eight siblings, only Charles and his brother Henry had children. Henry had a daughter named Mary W. Leaman (1888-1963), while Charles had two daughters, Mary A. ("China Mary") Leaman (1879-1972) and Lucy A. Leaman (1881-1968). These three women were the last heirs of the Leaman property at Leaman Place. Christiana Tsai (1890-1984) was later added to their deed before the land was deeded to AFC in 1966.

THE FORMATIVE YEARS OF CHARLES LEAMAN

Charles Leaman, born on September 3, 1845, was the seventh child of Henry and Catherine Amanda Leaman. He grew up surrounded by the vibrant life of Leaman Place. At the onset of the American Civil War in 1861, a young and patriotic Charles, just 16, was deemed too young to enlist. Despite discouragement from his father and his brother Henry, who was then a medical student and acting medic cadet at Jefferson Medical College, Charles's resolve remained unshaken. In December 1862, driven by his fervor to serve, he secretly left home. Guided by a local Navy recruitment ad, he made his way to Philadelphia, where he audaciously joined the Marine Corps, using a forged signature of his father to enlist. Later, his father reluctantly blessed him for his patriotism.

Figure 24: Charles Leaman in 1874.

Figure 25: The Admiral's Guard

In the Navy, Charles served as guard to Admiral John Dahlgren, the esteemed leader of the Naval Sea Force. During his nearly three years of military service, he penned 93 letters to his sister Mary, sharing vivid insights from the war. These correspondences were later captured in Donald L. Collin's historical novel, *The Admiral's Guard,* preserving his experiences for posterity.

Post-war, Charles returned to Leaman Place, where he encountered a transformative book titled *The Chinese Empire,* adorned with detailed engravings and narratives of China's history. This book, gifted by a friend, ignited his missionary zeal toward China.

EARLY CHINESE MIGRATION AND CHARLES'S CALLING

Long before the Civil War, Chinese immigrants began arriving in the US, primarily as merchants, sailors, and laborers. During the California Gold Rush from 1848 to 1855, many sought quick fortunes, while a devastating crop failure in southern China in 1852 drove over 20,000 migrants to San Francisco in search of better lives. By the late 1850s, these immigrants constituted a fifth of the population in Southern Mines' four counties.

From 1863 to 1869, the Central Pacific Railroad employed over 15,000 Chinese laborers to construct the first transcontinental railroad, significantly contributing to the development of California's agriculture and fisheries. Yet, these migrants faced intense racial discrimination, which escalated with the enactment of the Chinese Exclusion Act in 1882, deepening local animosity.

During this period, the global missionary movement was gaining momentum. Christian denominations, driven by evangelical fervor, sought to spread their faith worldwide. Missionary societies focused on regions like China, which was seen as a vast and ripe field for evangelism due to its large, relatively unreached population.

One of Charles Leaman's friends, Grace Biddle, whom he met through a family friend during his time in the Marine Corps, gifted him a book titled The Chinese Empire. This exquisite volume, adorned with 70 original full-page steel engravings and descriptive letterpress, hails from the era of Queen Victoria's reign. According to Charles's daughter, China Mary, it was this very book that ignited his early fascination with China. Over a century later, China Mary shared this book and its story with Leona Choy in their homestead attic. Grace Biddle had gone to China to teach before Charles, and her letters further fueled his interest in the country.

Through this captivating book and the inspiring letters from his friend who had already ventured to China, Charles felt a divine call to aid the Chinese people. He decided to leave his affluent family home and the legacy of four generations to spread the gospel in China.

At the tender age of 29, freshly ordained and armed with degrees from Princeton University and Union Theological Seminary, Charles bid heartfelt goodbyes to his beloved parents and siblings. They adored him deeply, knowing this farewell might be their last. Embracing the uncertainty with courage, Charles embarked on his destined path, ready to face whatever lay ahead.

In 1874, Charles embarked on his voyage across the Pacific, braving a month of tumultuous seas, and arrived in China determined to share the gospel. His journey marked a significant chapter in the Leaman family's history, starkly contrasting with the influx of Chinese immigrants to America seeking fortunes.

THE ESTABLISHMENT OF NANKING'S FIRST PRESBYTERIAN MISSION STATION

In 1874, Charle sarrived in Nanking, ready to join forces with the pioneering missionaries, Mr. and Mrs. Albert Whiting, who had settled there in 1873. Faced with local suspicions that cast foreigners in the light of invaders, the Whitings found themselves making a home on a humble houseboat outside the city's ancient walls—a creative response to the challenging circumstances.

Determined to bridge the cultural gap, Charles immersed himself in mastering the intricate Chinese language. As a sharp Princeton graduate, his aptitude for mastering Chinese was remarkable. This skill enabled him to join Mr. Whiting in roadside gatherings beside the busy streets and delve into meaningful conversations in bustling tea houses—places akin to American bars where locals hung out. There, they shared the gospel.

Charles fully embraced the local way of life, wearing traditional Chinese attire, growing his hair into a queue, and navigating the narrow streets on a motorcycle. His fluency in the language and unique style won him the nickname "China Charley," and he was affectionately known among the locals as Man Li 李满.

When the opportunity arose to purchase land for a permanent mission, local laws initially barred them as foreigners from owning property. However, a unique opportunity presented itself with a plot of land available for sale—a site once a battlefield, now shrouded in superstition and believed to be haunted. The locals avoided it, leaving it untouched and unwanted.

The magistrate, noting their interest, dryly commented, "If you want this land, you can go and live with the devils there." Undeterred by its eerie reputation, they eagerly seized the chance and, in 1876, established Nanking's first Presbyterian mission station on this very land.

This new mission station, built upon a land steeped in myths and spirits, became the 10th mission station in China, joining others that had been set up since the first was founded in Canton in 1815, followed by Ningbo in 1845, and Shanghai in 1850.

THE TRIUMPHS AND TRIALS IN NANKING

In the late 1870s, Charles's missionary journey in China took an unexpected turn when he met Miss Lucy A. Crouch, a fellow Presbyterian missionary from New Jersey. Born in Washington County, Pennsylvania, Lucy shared Charles's dedication to service. They married on December 10, 1878, merging their lives and missions.

In 1879, while in Shanghai, the couple welcomed their first daughter, Mary Amanda Leaman, followed by their second daughter, Lucy Atkinson Leaman, in 1881. Amid the bustling life of Shanghai, their family grew, deeply rooted in their love, commitment to each other, and their shared calling.

However, life in Nanking was fraught with hardship for them and the Whiting couple, with stressful work and challenging living conditions. In 1879, tragedy struck as Mr. Albert Whiting, Mr. Leaman's close friend and fellow missionary, passed away from illness, just six years after arriving in Nanking. Around the same time, Mrs. Leaman fell seriously ill, prompting Mr. and Mrs. Leaman to return to the US to seek medical treatment for her.

The 1879 Annual Report of the Board of Foreign Missions of the Presbyterian Church (BFMPC) detailed their struggles: "The Nanking mission station faced significant challenges, with a lack of resources delaying the construction of a church, even though the land of the battleground was purchased in 1876. Despite appeals for more laborers, the mission struggled due to insufficient recruits. Rev. Charles Leaman, the only ordained missionary at the station, had to obtain leave of absence due to his wife Lucy's health issues, and he was returning to US."

During the tumultuous period, Mr. Leaman temporarily served at the Hangchow Mission Station, assisting Rev. Samuel Dodd with the Hangchow Presbyterian Boy School and briefly overseeing it as superintendent. When additional missionaries arrived, Mr. and Mrs. Leaman returned to Nanking, where they became central figures at the mission station for the remainder of their time in China. With the support of other missionaries and local Chinese Christians, they established Nanking's first church, named "Four Poles," which accommodated 100 people.[2]

Mr. Leaman persevered in his preaching and chapel responsibilities, encouraged by the expanding congregations in Nanking, as reported in the 1883 annual report of BFMPC. Mr. Leaman reported the following:

> Our street chapel efforts have suffered from a lack of support, though significant outreach occurs on Sabbaths. We strive to

2 "Mochou Lu Church." Nanjing Travel, April 6, 2022. https://www.gonanjingchina.com/explore-nanjing-china/nanjing-travel-blog/nanjing-history-culture-and-religion/nanjing-religion/mochou-lu-church.

This the front gate of Yien Liao Fang Church
where Christiana has been working as an evangelist
since 1914. This Church was built by Uncle Charley.
Don't forget to pray for the electric
light!

Figure 26: This is the church built by Charles Leaman and what is on the back of photo.

> connect with the diverse crowds that pass through Nanking, including students, young policemen, and soldiers, all eager for new experiences. Yet, our resources are stretched thin, and the city's vast needs exceed our capacity. Despite the onset of new societal trends, traditional heathen practices still dominate every stratum of society, from the Governor General to the humblest beggar.

There were four street chapels, some crowded in fair weather and others working with less interest. Mr. Leaman wrote:

"The work of evangelization in the city has not been neglected, but our force is inadequate to the needs of our work in every way, and it has fallen far short in the evangelization of our large and important city. All the difficulties known at home in any city are here, and in addition, there is no help from a Christian civilization ruling in it. In all the sham of the new civilization springing up heathen cus-

Figure 27: Charles Leaman (the second from left) in Nanking, China.

toms and life predominate in all classes, from the Governor General down to the lowest beggar."

By 1888, Mr. Leaman had helped build a larger formal church, initially called "Jesus Church," accommodating 400 people. Renamed "Hangzhou Church" in 1927, it was later demolished for a road-widening project in 1934 but was rebuilt by Rev. Paul Abbott in a Gothic style in 1936, expanding its capacity to 1,000. In 1954, it was named "Mochou Road Church."

Today, Mochou Road Church is among the four major churches in Nanking, boasting 4,000 members and hosting nine different services and gatherings weekly. Around 2,000 congregants attend Sunday services regularly, with baptism ceremonies held biannually before Christmas and Easter.[3]

---

3 Yi, Yang. "Mochoulu Church of Nanking to Celebrate Her 80th Anniv. with Revival Gathering." China Christian Daily. Accessed October 21, 2022. https://chinachristiandaily.com/news/church_ministry/2016-08-29/mochoulu-church-of-nanking-to-celebrate-her-80th-anniv--with-revival-gathering-_2270.

THE BOXER REBELLION

In 1898, as China grappled with severe natural disasters and rising social unrest, the Boxer Rebellion began to take shape. Named for their martial prowess, the Boxers were a fervent group, drawn from peasants, idle youths, and former soldiers, who united under a common cause—to expel foreign influence, which they believed brought calamity upon their land.

In these perilous times, Christian missionaries Mr. and Mrs. Leaman found themselves targets of the Boxers' wrath. One dire afternoon, a mob seized Mr. Leaman, binding him with ropes to throw him into a canal. At the last moment, Mrs. Leaman, alerted by her Chinese friends, rushed to the scene, arriving just in time to thwart the grim fate awaiting her husband.

On another occasion, the menacing clang of the Big Sword Society's weapons signaled another attack. As the mob advanced on their home one stormy night, a sudden flooding stalled their progress, buying precious time for the Leamans to escape. Fleeing in sedan chairs through a back door, they narrowly missed the rioters who stormed their front entrance.

Meanwhile, a crucial decision lay with Mr. Sung Hua Tsai, the Acting Viceroy of Nanking and father of Christiana Tsai. The Empress Dowager, capitalizing on the Boxers' fervor, had decreed the extermination of all foreigners to quash the uprising. In a bold act of defiance, Mr. Tsai covertly altered her orders from slaughter to protection, risking execution for himself and his family if discovered.

At home, the gravity of his decision weighed heavily as Mr. Tsai confided in his wife, fearing for their lives and the lives of their 24 children and numerous servants. Despite the risks, they chose to stay, and their decision saved countless lives, including Mr. and Mrs. Leaman. Nanking remained a safe haven, even as other regions succumbed to violence.

The Boxer Rebellion led to the brutal deaths of at least 189 foreign missionaries, including 53 children, especially under the harsh policies of Shansi's governor, Yuxian.[4] Yet, the courage and resolve of people like Mr. Leaman and Mr. Tsai highlighted the complexities of this tumultuous period.

After China's defeat in 1900, the Qing government was compelled to sign the Boxer Protocol in 1901, agreeing to heavy reparations and increased concessions to foreign powers. In an unexpected turn, some of these funds were redirected into a gesture of goodwill: the Boxer Indemnity Scholarship Program. This initiative enabled around 1,300 Chinese students to study in the US, paving the way for the establishment of Tsinghua University, now a pillar of modern Chinese education.

The Boxer Rebellion, with its stark contrasts of terror and bravery, profoundly influenced China's historical trajectory and its global interactions, forging paths of resistance, endurance, and healing amidst formidable challenges.

Founded in 1911, the scholarship program's preparatory school evolved into the prestigious Tsinghua University. Many notable Chinese and Chinese Americans have emerged from this program, highlighting its significant and enduring impact.

THE FIRST GIRLS' SCHOOL IN NANKING

In ancient China, societal norms held that "A woman's virtue is without talent" and "A woman's strength lies in her ignorance." These beliefs confined women to roles of marriage and motherhood, discouraging them from seeking education. The thought was that literacy might morally corrupt women. Thus, a woman's chastity and self-sacrifice were prized, and female literacy was viewed with suspicion and

4 Huang, Xipei. In Remembrance of Martyrs a Century Ago: Records and Documents Related to Missionary Martyrs of the 1900 Boxer Incident.

disdain. Many parents hesitated to educate their daughters, fearing that knowledge could lead them astray.

Foot-binding was another grim practice stemming from the idea that women should remain inside the home. This crippling tradition was so widespread that unbound women were derisively called "big boats" and had a hard time finding husbands. Women with bound feet were essentially immobilized, needing to be carried in sedan chairs for any travel, reinforcing their domestic confinement.

In 1884, amidst strong cultural opposition, Mr. and Mrs. Leaman founded the Ming Deh Girls' School in Nanking, yet faced a discouraging start with not a single student enrolling in the first three months. Mrs. Leaman, however, was undeterred. Having previously taught at the True Light School in Canton; she was well acquainted with the challenges of introducing education in resistant environments.

Figure 28: The Ming Deh Girls School in Nanking

True Light, a missionary boarding school founded in 1872 by her friend Miss Harriet Newell Noyes, had initially struggled as well, starting with only six students despite offering free meals and accommodation. Over 15 years, through persistent effort and dedication, the school's enrollment rose to 100 students. Armed with this experience, Mrs. Leaman remained steadfast, committed to her vision for the Ming Deh Girls' School in Nanking.

Persistence paid off at Ming Deh too. The school's first pupil appeared three months after opening, but she was reluctant to learn, attending only to play and eat. When formal learning began, she fled and never returned. The second student, a gatekeeper's daughter, had to be paid to attend classes.

Mrs. Leaman, undeterred, continued her mission with unwavering faith. Over time, as missionaries increasingly engaged in China, preaching and establishing schools and hospitals, and advocating against practices like foot-binding and opium addiction, Christian influence slowly gained acceptance. Enrollment at Ming Deh gradually improved.

Among the students was Su Juan, later known as Christiana Tsai, the daughter of the Acting Viceroy. She embraced Christianity and became a pivotal figure in spreading the faith. Her extraordinary life and profound impact will be explored in greater detail later.

A QUARTER CENTURY OF GROWTH: THE FOUNDER'S REFLECTION

In 1909, as Ming Deh Girls' School marked its 25th anniversary, Mrs. Leaman took a moment to reflect on the remarkable journey since the school's inception. Her words capture the profound transformation from the school's humble beginnings to its flourishing present:

Figure 29: Lucy Leaman

> "Looking at the Nanking of today, with more than 300 girls in its 5 Mission schools, one can hardly realize the difficulties faced by the one who in October 1884, with the building, teacher, books, food, and cook all in readiness, opened the first girls' school in this city

and waited for the children whose fears were more than good food and clothing could calm.

It is a small wonder that the children were afraid when the mothers hardly dared enter one of the rooms for fear of a trap door into which they might suddenly disappear, and the fathers scarcely had courage enough to taste food in a foreign house.

Several days after the school was open one lone little girlie ventured in. She was allowed to eat the school rice, but she slept at home, probably so the effect of her contact with foreigners could be better watched. Three days passed, and Mrs. Leaman hardly dared to look at the child lest it frighten her away.

What a contrast—this lone, unwilling student—when we see her beside the 8 girls who, on their commencement day, marched up the aisle of the church with two lines of admiring schoolmates standing on each side. The more than 300 guests entertained in the schoolyard by the girls at their commencement tea this year, absolutely fearless, most interested, and appreciative, were very different from the timid friends that visited the same school so many years ago.

A class of 8 was graduated in May, all Christians, all desiring to serve their Master. One takes up evangelistic work, two will teach in the schools, one married an evangelist, one a Christian businessman, who is letting her help us this year, while the other three remain with us as teachers.

The revival meetings in February brought changes that we sorrowfully feel we had not faith to hope for. Confession of sins, some ordinarily called trivial and not before recognized as sin, came from many. Small thefts of yarn for their hair, etc., lying, failure to use opportunities to make Christ known, cheating in examinations, talking in the schoolroom during study hour, unkind criticism, and pouting troubled many.

> Things done in ill-temper, things done thoughtlessly, unkind things said and done in fun, oh! the suffering they caused, when in His love the Savior gave them to see sin just a little bit as it is in the Father's sight! Girls whose proud, stubborn, suspicious hearts had been so hard to touch, girls we had all but despaired of, were in those days made new.
>
> All the girls of 6 classes either came for the first time or took a new stand. With the exception of two, all who did not were either too little or had not been in long.
>
> The kindergarten children were very much interested and many were deeply touched. Several tots knocked at the door one day and asked to be taught to pray. The crowning blessing came on the last Sabbath before the parting for summer vacation, when 15 girls were taken into the church.
>
> As they stood there at the close of the twenty-fifth year, what a token they seemed of fulfilled promises, what a previous earnest of coming blessings!"

THE ENDURING LEGACY OF LUCY LEAMAN IN NANKING

In 1910, at the ages of 64 and 60 respectively, Mr. and Mrs. Leaman returned to Paradise for a furlough with their daughters Mary, 24, and Lucy, 21. Tragically, shortly after their return to China, Mrs. Leaman passed away in Kuling, China, on October 9, 1910.

A close friend and fellow missionary, Mrs. Williams, penned a heartfelt tribute to Mrs. Leaman:

> "Coming with her husband to Nanking, they worked through hard, strenuous years, laying the foundations for our work. Teaching, preaching, studying, a loving mother, a careful housekeeper, given to hospitality, her work knew no bounds.

As the years went by people went to her for sympathy-new missionaries, perplexed and troubled ones of every Mission, the school-girls, the men of the church, the little tap-tap on her door as some little school-girl or some burdened woman came with her story, ate into her resting times, yet she gave to all unselfishly.

Many people have said that the peace and harmony of our working community is largely due to the influence of Mr. and Mrs. Leaman. In our first six months in China we, as new missionaries living in their home, heard no unkind story or criticism of any fellow workers.

Figure 30: Charles in China in 1919.

The Chinese were their adopted people, and so no story of their evil or dishonesty came to us, but instead instances of their fidelity and little heart stories of their struggles won our sympathy."

Mrs. Leaman devoted her life to missionary work in Nanking, China, where she served as an educator and spiritual guide. Renowned for her kindness and dedication, Mrs. Leaman's impact on the community was profound, leaving a legacy of respect and affection from those she helped and inspired. Her contributions continue to resonate, deeply embedded in the fabric of the community.

CHARLES LEAMAN'S FINAL COMMITMENT TO CHINA

Rev. Charles Leaman dedicated the years from 1878 to 1881 to his mission in Hangchow and from 1881 to 1920 in Nanking. In 1920,

Figure 31: Charles's memorial service in China in 1920.

Figure 32: Charles's gravesite is behind the gate.

he returned to his homeland for a well-deserved furlough. Tragically, shortly after resuming his service in China, he passed away in Nanking from cerebral apoplexy on December 2, 1920, at the age of 75.

Despite his advanced age and declining health, Mr. Leaman's decision to return to China underscored his profound commitment to the people and the land he had dedicated his life to serving. Mr. Leaman was laid to rest in the Chinese Presbyterian Cemetery at Tsiag Liang Shan, a poignant testament to his enduring devotion.

"Very truly I tell you, unless a kernel of wheat falls to the ground and dies, it remains only a single seed. But if it dies, it produces many seeds." (John 12:24)

God used Mr. and Mrs. Leaman as seeds planted in China to reach countless souls, including Christiana Tsai. Over 100 years later, by divine inspiration, AFC's headquarters was established on his homeland property, continuing to reach Chinese people for Christ.

Mr. and Mrs. Leaman's journey illuminates the pivotal role of foreign missions in driving crucial societal changes—from advancing women's education to eradicating foot-binding in China. Their dedicated service exemplifies the profound impact that unwavering missionary commitment can have on a culture.

From the humble beginnings of the "Four Poles" church, established by Rev. Charles Leaman and his fellow missionaries on battleground land purchased in 1876, a sanctuary that could accommodate only 100 people, it has now grown into one of the four largest churches in Nanking. Today, it boasts 4,000 members and hosts nine different services and gatherings weekly.

The story of Mr. and Mrs. Leaman serves as a powerful testament to God's unending faithfulness—a steadfast promise that fortifies us today and guides us into all our tomorrows.

Chapter 4

MARY LEAMAN AND CHRISTIANA TSAI

MARY LEAMAN'S PATH TO MISSIONARY SERVICE

In the pulsing center of Shanghai, where life teemed with vigor and spirit, Mary Amanda Leaman (known in Chinese as 李美玲, and affectionately called China Mary) first opened her eyes to the world on October 8, 1879. Born to Rev. Charles and Mrs. Lucy Leaman, fervent missionaries, she was embraced by a life rich with spiritual destiny from her very first breath. Following closely in her path, her sister Lucy A. Leaman was born on November 6, 1881. Together, the sisters grew, cradled by the vibrant rhythms of this bustling Chinese metropolis. Yet, young Mary's early years were shadowed by adversity. When she was just three years old, a severe fall inflicted a lasting burden—an injured spine that would persist as a lifelong challenge.

This chapter's content was heavily drawn from the autobiography of Christiana Tsai, as recounted in her book:Tsai, Christiana. *Queen of the Dark Chamber: The Story of Christiana Tsai*. Paradise, PA: Ambassadors for Christ Inc., 1986; and Leaman, Ivan B. "The Remarkable Leaman Family of Leaman Place." Mennonite Life, January 2017.

Despite this formidable obstacle, the indomitable spirits of Mary and her sister Lucy shone brightly. Their resilience was unwavering, steadfast against the trials they faced.

Figure 33: Young Mary Leaman

The sisters' upbringing, steeped in the rich tapestries of Chinese culture, eventually took a turn toward the familiar soil of America. For their high school education, they traveled across the oceans to Wooster, Ohio, where they found a second home at the Westminster Mission Home—a sanctuary for the daughters of missionaries. This home, a melting pot of stories and backgrounds, housed many young women who, like Mary and Lucy, were born under foreign skies.

Within the nurturing confines of Westminster, Mary's spinal condition intensified, compelling her to seek solace in the tranquil surroundings of Markleton Sanatorium in Pennsylvania. On September 9, 1899, doctors diagnosed her with a curvature of the spine. Yet, even as her physical struggles mounted, her spirit remained undeterred, resilient in the face of adversity.

At the age of twenty, Mary Leaman felt a divine summons echoing deep within her soul, compelling her to join her parents in their missionary work in China. In 1899, she eagerly submitted her application to the Women's Foreign Missionary Society of the Presbyterian Church. A glowing recommendation accompanied her submission, penned by Sylvia Anderson from Westminster Home, who praised Mary's nurturing spirit: "Mary is a beautiful Christian Character. She has always been a comfort and help to us in the Home."

In July of the same year, Mary expressed her heartfelt intention in a letter to Ann Perkins, conveying her "desire to take the Gospel of

Salvation to those in darkness and [to] join my dear mother in her work in Christ." By August, she was planning her next steps, deciding to attend the normal school in West Chester. There, she hoped to gain invaluable skills for missionary service, should it be God's will to call her abroad.

By December 1899, the principal of West Chester Normal School, George Morris Philips, endorsed Mary's readiness, noting her as a "young woman of fine manners and appearance, attractive in every way, a faithful student and consistent Christian. She is a little timid and yet active and faithful in Christian work. It is my belief that she will make a faithful and efficient Christian worker in any field."

With her path now clear, Mary received the official approval from the Women's Foreign Missionary Society in January 1900. Fulfilling her calling, she set sail for China on May 27, 1901, and by June 20, she was once again on Chinese soil, ready to weave her life into the fabric of her spiritual calling.

FROM ADVERSITY TO EMPOWERMENT: OVERCOMING OBSTACLES AT MING DEH GIRLS' SCHOOL

Mary and Lucy Leaman joined their parents on an impactful venture at the Ming Deh Girls' School in Nanking, an institution their parents founded in 1884. Establishing the first girls' school in Nanking was an ambitious endeavor, fraught with challenges due to local cultural opposition.

Mary Leaman recounted the turbulent beginnings in her writings:

> The opening of school last year was not easy, as word came to us about three weeks before that both of our men teachers had been gambling. After inquiring into the matter, we felt very strongly that it was far better to have all the teaching done by the matron, the older girls and ourselves, rather than run any risk with teachers of whom we were not sure. Sending them off was hard, not simply because of the burden of work they

> left, but one had been in the school for twelve years, and the other had been in our boys' school from a little boy.
>
> At the opening of school, the girl who came back to us to teach, leaving a ten-dollar-a-month position for the one with us at five, came with a gift of ten dollars. She had received so much from the school, she said, that she wanted to give a little as a token of her gratitude.[5]

Amidst these early challenges, the commitment to education and the spirit of community within the school continued to grow, as reflected in a subsequent report:

> Kindergarten. -Miss Lucy Leaman, who has charge of the kindergarten, reports that the full seating capacity of the rooms was taxed this year by the 61 children enrolled, of whom 21 were day-pupils.

As time progressed, Mary ascended to the role of principal of Ming Deh Girls' School, with Lucy taking the helm of the kindergarten and supporting various facets of school operations. Together, they shaped a beacon of learning and hope in Nanking, steering their institution through initial adversities to nurture a legacy of education and empowerment for young girls.

CULTURAL CROSSROADS: SU JUAN (CHRISTIANA TSAI) AT MING DEH GIRLS' SCHOOL

On a radiant day in 1906, a luxury sedan chair halted at the gates of the Four Flagstaffs mission compound in Nanking, home to the

---

5 Presbyterian Church in the U.S.A. (Old School). "Annual Report of the Board of Foreign Missions of the Presbyterian Church, in the United States of America. 1907-1909." HathiTrust. Accessed September 29, 2022. https://babel.hathitrust.org/cgi/pt?id=coo.31924071141935&view=1up&seq=229&skin=2021&q1=Charles+Leaman.

Ming Deh Girls' School. From it emerged a 16-year-old girl adorned in lavish attire and embroidered shoes.

Greeting her was the school's young principal, 26-year-old Mary, dressed in a modest grey dress with black trim. Mary's calm demeanor and serene presence immediately impressed the newcomer. "I want to register in your school to learn English and play the piano," the girl declared.

"What is your name? Who are your parents? Where do you live?" Mary inquired softly.

"My father is Tsai Sung Hua. We reside on Millstone Street, and I am Tsai Ling Fang," she responded.

"Mr. Tsai, the Acting Viceroy?" Mary asked, visibly surprised. The girl nodded in confirmation.

Mary's expression grew serious, causing a flicker of fear in the girl.

"We would be very glad to have you come and learn English and piano, but we can't take you in as a boarder. Our school is very poor, and many of the students are orphans. Our food is very coarse, and our students do the housework. I fear that you would not enjoy living here since you are used to better things," Mary explained.

"Oh, yes, I would! I don't mind coarse food and poor people. I want to learn English," the girl insisted.

"But did your mother give you permission to come to our school?" Mary pressed.

"Oh, yes, indeed she did," the girl answered.

"Well, we have a rule that the parents must come here themselves and give us their permission for you to study. Can you ask your mother to come?" Mary suggested.

"I can try," said the girl before returning to her sedan chair and heading home.

The young girl, Su Juan Tsai, later known as Christiana Tsai, was the eighteenth child of the Vice Governor and the Acting Governor of Kiangsu Province. Born on February 12, 1890, she grew up in a sprawling family estate in Nanking, complete with large houses, beautiful gardens, and numerous servants. Despite the opulence, Su Juan felt a profound dissatisfaction with her sheltered life.

Chafing against the rigid cultural norms of her time, including the practice of foot-binding, Su Juan was driven by a deep desire to master English and immerse herself in the world of music, her true passion. Despite facing staunch resistance from her devout Buddhist parents, her resolve never wavered. Firm in her promise not to embrace Christianity, she gradually secured their grudging approval to attend the missionary school.

When Su Juan explained to her mother that she needed to personally give permission at the school, her mother initially resisted due to her busy schedule. Yet, Su Juan's persistent pleas swayed her, and she agreed to visit the school.

The next day there was a great commotion and intense excitement among the girls in the Ming Deh Girls' School when the Viceroy's wife and her daughter's sedan chair arrived at Ming Deh Girls' School in sequence. Su Juan's mother was very gracious and Mary was very polite. Their first encounter left both of them with a good impression of each other. So, Su Juan was approved to register as a day student at Ming Deh Girls' School.

Mary maintained that Su Juan could not board with the school's orphans. Instead, Su Juan's mother arranged for a private rickshaw and hired a driver to take her to school each day.

Su Juan eagerly immersed herself in English and piano lessons, consciously avoiding the English Bible class to respect her family's caution against adopting Christianity. However, her first experience of a Christmas service at the school and receiving her first Bible from Lucy Leaman as a Christmas gift sparked a flicker of curiosity, though she remained uncommitted to the faith at that moment.

Despite her family's warnings to steer clear of "eating Christianity," Su Juan's encounter with the festive celebration intrigued her. She attended the Christmas service, enveloped by its warmth and spirit, yet without fully grasping its significance. The gift of a Bible was a gesture of goodwill she appreciated, though its pages remained unexplored, her interest in its teachings not yet kindled.

FROM DEFIANCE TO DELIVERANCE: THE ARDUOUS PATH OF SU JUAN'S FAITH

Su Juan cherished her time at Ming Deh Girls' School, yet the lengthy daily rickshaw ride through the city left her exhausted. She soon transferred to a missionary school in Soochow designed for girls from affluent families, offering superior food and services, where she could board. There, she bonded with Miss Wu, a fellow student of similar background, both determined to avoid converting to Christianity despite the school's influences.

Su Juan's passion for learning English led her to a sermon by the esteemed American speaker S.D. Gordon, a moment that would leave a profound imprint on her heart. He spoke on "Jesus, the Light of the World," using an analogy that deeply resonated with her:

> If a piece of wood is kept in a dark place, all kinds of ugly insects will hide under it. But if we expose it to the light, the insects will run away, for they love darkness and hate the light. So it is with our hearts: if we do not have Jesus, the light of the world, in our hearts, they will be dark too and harbor all kinds of evil thoughts. The moment we receive Him and the light He brings, the evil thoughts will all be driven away.

This metaphor struck a chord with Su Juan, particularly because of her childhood fear of insects. This message came vividly to life one sunny day as she played croquet in the yard. She noticed a smooth white stone on the grass—Gordon's sermon echoing in her mind. Driven by curiosity, she tapped the stone with her mallet, flipping it over. Instantly, a host of bugs—a lizard, a centipede, and smaller insects—hurried away from the intrusion of light, and a voice inside her said, "You are just like this stone, smooth and white outside, and full of sin inside."

A beam of light came from God, and Su Juan suddenly saw the darkness in her own heart. She recalled that Mary often spoke of the importance of prayer. So, she hurried back to her own room, knelt down, and prayed for the first time. "Lord, forgive my sin and help me to understand Thy Word." After that, Su Juan opened her heart to Christianity and brought her best friend Miss Wu to Christ. Together, they embraced belief, finding serene peace in their newfound devotion.

When their families discovered they had embraced Christianity, the reaction was explosive. Miss Wu's family was so outraged that they dispatched a relative to collect her and her belongings from school.

On the journey home, this relative presented her with a knife and a rope, threatening, "You have disgraced your family by eating the Christian religion. Didn't we warn you not to listen to it? Your family is very angry and does not want you as their daughter anymore. If you do not promise to give up your Christianity now and return to our religion, you will have to choose between this rope to hang yourself, this knife to stab yourself, or the canal to drown yourself."

Miss Wu's face color almost looked like white paper. But with quiet determination, she said "I cannot give up Jesus. He died for my sins to open for me the way to Heaven. I belong to Him. You may take my life; you cannot harm my soul." Her relative was awed by her determination and did not force her to commit suicide. Returning to her home, Miss Wu endured her family members' angry accusations and cruel punishment, but she remained true to Christ.

When Su Juan's conversion to Christianity came to light, her family's response was vehement. Upon her return, her mother wept bitterly at the sight of her, and her sixth brother erupted in anger. "You have disgraced the whole family! We meant you to get an education, not to eat this foreign religion!" he exclaimed. In his fury, he grabbed the Bible from Su Juan, tearing it to shreds and throwing the pieces at her.

Su Juan was stunned; her family had always treated each other with respect. But Su Juan said nothing to them and silently looked to God. Suddenly, she saw a vision of Christ on the cross, a crown of thorns on His head and with nails in His hands. Su Juan knew that God had suffered for our sins; He purchased our heads with His crown and our hands with His nails. There was nothing she could not bear for God as Jesus had suffered so much for us. She remained silent but her faith was even stronger than before.

Realizing they couldn't sway Su Juan's steadfast faith, her family determined to keep her at home, barring her from returning to school. Despite their mockery and ridicule, Su Juan maintained her composure. Amidst the tension, her eighth brother, showing more warmth than the others, invited her to collaborate on a project—translating Charles Dickens's *A Tale of Two Cities* into Chinese. During this shared endeavor, Su Juan led her brother to embrace Christianity.

This revelation infuriated her mother even further. In despair, she exclaimed, "I can't bear this! It's bad enough my daughter follows this religion, but my son too? I might as well send her away, marry her off to preserve our family's honor. But you, my son, I rely on you for my rites when I pass. You must not speak to her!" Overwhelmed by her emotions, Su Juan's mother wept continuously for seven days and seven nights, grappling with the shifting beliefs within her family.

Then Su Juan was given fine clothes in order to be married off, but Su Juan looked at the finery and told her mother, "Jesus is more to me than anything on earth! I cannot do this." Her mother finally saw the futility of keeping her a prisoner at home and said to her, "I won't keep you here to delude your brothers with your Christianity religion. You must return to your school and finish your schooling there." Therefore, Su Juan went back to her school, excelled and graduated with distinction.

Upon the completion of her high school education, Su Juan stood at a crossroads paved with prestigious offers: to ascend to the position of vice principal of her alma mater, to serve as the general secretary of the YWCA, and to journey as a traveling lecturer advocating for women's education—an exceptional honor, considering she was among the rare few Chinese women of her era educated in the Western tradition.

Yet amidst these tempting prospects, Su Juan discerned a distinct call from God—a beckoning to return to her roots in Nanking and bear witness to His love. With a heart aligned with divine purpose, she declined the worldly honors and set her sights on her familial home, determined to kindle the flame of faith within her loved ones.

Upon her return, Su Juan sought out Mary Leaman, the esteemed principal of Ming Deh Girls' School, with a proposition that was both humble and audacious. "Would you like to have me help you in the evangelistic work?" she inquired gently. Mary, startled yet delighted by such an offer from a woman as distinguished as Su Juan, eagerly accepted. With this, Su Juan made the decision to stay at her family home, wholeheartedly committing to the spiritual mission alongside Mary.

Su Juan's foremost mission was to guide her mother to embrace Christ. Despite her fervent efforts, her mother remained staunch, even declaring, "Only when I am dead, encased in my coffin with the lid securely fastened, will I consider your Jesus." But the Lord works in mysterious ways, often weaving paths through the stoniest hearts. Su Juan remained steadfast, trusting in God's gentle power to transform even the most resolute disbelief.

FAITH AMIDST THE FLAMES: DIVINE DELIVERANCE IN NANKING

In the shadow of Nanking's invasion, as marauding Japanese forces neared, Su Juan's household plunged into panic. The invaders, notorious for their brutality, hammered at the gates of her stately home.

A house servant ran to Su Juan and fearfully announced, "They are searching for the master and mistress of the house! They hang them and beat them, doing terrible things until they give them everything. You must flee!"

"They are coming toward our house now! They are shooting at our iron gates!" another servant shouted.

Her servants, frantic with fear, urged escape through a concealed door. While her family fled, Su Juan faced a dire predicament—her elderly mother, hindered by bound feet and a freshly twisted ankle, implored her to flee and save herself.

"Daughter, I can't go on—I'm hurt! I will only slow everyone down, and then all will be caught and murdered. Go on without me. I am old and useless—go," her mother pleaded.

"No, Mother. I love you. You are precious to me—and to God!" Su Juan prayed under her breath, "O dear Lord, I claim all those promises I have just been reading. Protect us all. You promised that 'but it will not come near you' (Psalm 91:7b). Dear Jesus! Save us from this destruction!" She prayed, feeling a divine fortitude surge through her.

With the sword clanging against the iron gate and the feet kicking the massive doors, Su Juan suddenly gained unusual wisdom and strength from the Lord. She hoisted her mother to her back and staggered toward the rear entrance to the servants' quarters. "Jesus will help us," she assured, her voice a tremulous mix of fear and faith.

With bullets flying over their heads, she kicked open the back door of the servants' quarters and put her mother, who had nearly fainted in fear, into the cramped, dark place under the stairway. Then she crawled into this moldy, odor-filled space and held her mother in her lap. With the chill of a tomb, she whispered. "Mother, Mother, Jesus will help us. He promised!" Then she prayed with chattering teeth, "Lord, help me to be a good testimony for you. I am no use dead!"

As heavy footsteps of soldiers came within inches of them, Su Juan prayed more desperately, again pleading for the promises from the precious psalm which God had given her that morning:

"For he will command his angels concerning you to guard you in all your ways" (Psalm 91:11).

Finally, the heavy boots of those soldiers moved on. Su Juan and her mother escaped the disaster. When Su Juan's brothers and sisters crawled out of their hiding place, they were grief-stricken, supposing the worst, expecting to see their mother hanging mutilated by the soldiers. When they caught sight of Su Juan with their mother on her back, they ran crying and throwing themselves on the ground before them with relief and joy.

"It's God who has saved us," Su Juan whispered faintly. "Hurry and wipe the cobwebs from Mother's face, change her clothes, and soak her foot."

Su Juan's brothers were embarrassed about their own behavior and wondered how their sister had the courage to save their mother. They asked about her saying that the Lord had delivered them. Su Juan saw their unusual gentleness and the first flicker of seeking truth in their eyes. "Brothers, it is the only true, living God who can deliver us from trouble. Idols and incense are no use in the face of disaster. They can't save us. They cannot give us peace." Su Juan knew it would not be long before the Lord would bring more of her family into His kingdom.

The ongoing peril forced the Tsai family to leave Nanking for Shanghai. Amidst a tumultuous crowd, Su Juan, still bearing her mother, joined the throng heading for safety. Once in Shanghai, the physical and emotional toll weighed heavily on her, but even in her exhaustion, her family marveled at her resilience—attributing it to her steadfast faith in Jesus.

Su Juan's courage and unwavering faith not only saved her mother but also planted seeds of belief in her family's hearts, paving the way for their eventual embrace of the faith. Through her actions, they witnessed the profound impact of a living God capable of delivering them from the depths of despair.

BREAKING CHAINS: THE JOURNEY OF CHRISTIANA TSAI'S MOTHER FROM ADDICTION TO REDEMPTION

In the bustling city of Nanking, as the winds of change ushered in the Republic of China, a stringent law was enacted to curb the scourge of opium. Amidst this transformative era, Su Juan's mother, ensnared by the relentless grip of opium addiction, faced a daunting challenge. Fearful of the new regulations, she resolved to conquer her dependence on the drug.

Compelled by her daughter's gentle persuasions, she sought refuge in a Quaker hospital renowned for its compassionate care. What followed were two harrowing weeks marked by intense withdrawal symptoms and a complete loss of appetite. Yet, in her darkest hours, she was not alone. Miss Mary Leaman, a devoted nurse and principal of Ming Deh Girls' School, became a beacon of hope. Mary fasted, prayed, and regularly brought flowers and nourishing meals to Su Juan's mother, embodying the love and patience of the ministry they served.

Driven to desperation, Su Juan's mother made a solemn plea: "If your Jesus will take away this appetite, I will believe him." To which Su Juan, steadfast in faith, replied, "Don't say 'if'—believe that He will." That night, a life-altering vision occurred. Jesus appeared, enveloped in a radiant, divine light that seemed to wrap her in its brilliance. This encounter marked a pivotal victory. Swept up in a sudden wave of intense perspiration, her longing for opium dissipated completely.

After she returned from the hospital, Su Juan's mother announced, "It was Jesus who answered the prayers of Miss Leaman and healed me." She urged, "My wish is that all my children and I will serve the Living God."

With renewed vigor, she shattered the idols in their family temple, and gave the most valuable idol of Tsai's family temple that had a pearl headdress and lungs and a gold heart, which Tsai's family had kept for over one hundred years, to Miss Mary Leaman and said "This is a keepsake for you. You have helped me to turn from idols and believe in Jesus. You should have it to show that the Tsai family idols have all been destroyed." The ripple effect of her transformation was profound. Alongside six family members, she was baptized in a chapel built by Rev. Charlie Leaman.

Captivated by the allegorical depths of John Bunyan's *Pilgrim's Progress,* Su Juan felt a profound connection to the protagonist's spiritual journey. In homage, she chose the name Christiana Tsai, marking a pivotal transformation in her identity. From that moment, she would be known as Christiana, and her spiritual mentor, previously referred to as Mary, would be honored as Miss Leaman.

The warmth and faith of Christiana's household continued to grow, especially after her mother's conversion. The first missionary she welcomed was Miss Leaman, who brought with her a gift as unique as the bond they shared—an unusually large hen known for its double-yoked eggs. This simple yet profound gift symbolized the extraordinary blessings and abundance their faith would bring.

One day, when Miss Leaman and Christiana were together doing Bible study, Christiana's mother called Miss Leaman, "Miss Leaman, I don't know how to express my gratitude to you for leading our family to find the true God through Jesus Christ. Would you accept my seventh daughter to be your daughter in the Lord?" From then on, Miss Leaman and Christiana accepted this beautiful relationship and they stayed together for 58 years! Christiana Tsai referred to Miss Mary Leaman as her Godmother.

With her family's blessing, Christiana eventually left her home to forge her own spiritual path, inspired by the teachings and love she had received. Her journey was a testament to the power of faith to transform lives and to the grace that guides the faithful through their pilgrimages in this world.

SPREADING LIGHT: CHRISTIANA TSAI'S MISSIONARY JOURNEY FROM CHINA TO THE WHITE HOUSE

Milton Stewart, an American millionaire deeply committed to his faith, donated $3 million for global evangelical efforts, with a significant portion directed toward China. This generous contribu-

Figure 34: Young Christiana Tsai

tion facilitated the visits of esteemed American Christian leaders to China, where Christiana Tsai served as their interpreter. Together, they delivered sermons across the nation, addressing large gatherings in cities and smaller, diverse crowds in the countryside. When existing venues couldn't accommodate the throngs, tents were swiftly erected.

Their journeys took them through China's vast landscapes—by rail, riverboat, coastal steamer, sedan chair, wheelbarrow, houseboat, and rickshaw. Despite facing numerous challenges and opposition, they were protected by divine grace, leading countless individuals from various backgrounds to embrace Christianity.

From 1914 to 1920, Christiana traveled across 11 of China's 18 provinces, working closely with luminaries like Miss Ruth Paxson, Dr. Griffith Thomas, and Dr. Charles Trumbull. She translated Paxson's work, *Rivers of Living Water,* into Chinese and was instrumental in spreading Paxson's teachings, interpreting for her around three hundred times.

The extensive travels opened Christiana's eyes to the urgent needs for mass education and evangelical work in China, inspiring her to establish the first Chinese Home Missionary Society. Through this organization, funds were raised to send six missionaries to the southwestern province of Yunnan, aiming to reach minority groups with the gospel.

Later, Christiana took up a position as a music teacher at Jiangsu Girls' Normal School, a government-sponsored institution. Her influence was profound, leading 72 of the 2,000 students to Christianity. Despite facing persecution from both the school authorities and the students' families, Christiana and her converts remained steadfast in their faith.

In her spare time, Christiana devoted herself to visiting hospitals and running half-day schools for women, where she taught them to read and write Chinese characters. Her efforts not only spread the Christian faith but also empowered many through education and personal care.

In 1921, during Miss Leaman's return to the US for her furlough, she brought Christiana Tsai along for her first visit to America. Christiana was struck by the abundant resources and freedoms enjoyed in the US. During her stay, Christiana embarked on a speaking tour, captivating audiences with her insights and experiences. Her compelling presentations even led to an invitation to the White House by President Warren G. Harding. During her visit, she presented the President with a cherished ink box, a prestigious gift once given to her father by the former Chinese emperor. President Harding greatly appreciated this thoughtful and historic gesture.

FAITHFUL ENDEAVORS: MISS LEAMAN'S PHONETIC BIBLE MISSION

After the passing of Christiana's father, her family downsized to a smaller courtyard home. Although Christiana's mother invited Miss Leaman to move in with them, Miss Leaman chose a nearby house built by the Tsai family close to the chapel. Despite suffering from a painful spinal condition that kept her from public preaching, Miss Leaman remained a pivotal spiritual force, often engaging in deep prayer and conceptual thinking. During her travels across China for meetings, she had to be carried while lying flat due to her condition.

Miss Leaman played a crucial role in pushing Christiana beyond her comfort zone into public ministry—a role Christiana initially resisted. "But Godmother, I don't want to," she would protest. Miss Leaman would reply pointedly, "Suppose you had a pen that refused to write. Would you stop writing? Of course not. You would change to another one. You can't change God's plan by refusing to be as He asks. He will change to another instrument, and you will lose your opportunity!"

In 1930, as the Chinese National Government introduced a new phonetic system to complement traditional Chinese script, Miss Leaman saw the chance to fulfill a cherished dream of her late father: to translate the entire Bible, both Old and New Testaments, into phonetic characters, making it accessible to the illiterate. Inspired by a friend's sudden donation of two thousand dollars for a mass education program, Miss Leaman embarked on the ambitious project of transcribing the Bible, placing phonetic characters alongside traditional Chinese characters.

Figure 35: Mary Leaman and Christiana Tsai

Despite her retirement and physical ailments, Miss Leaman was determined to oversee this monumental task. She hired an experienced printer and two apprentices, securing an office in Shanghai for the operation. She meticulously proofread the text while her team handled the casting, typesetting, and printing. The Bible Society later took on the publishing duties.

Even in retirement and despite enduring constant pain, Miss Leaman's unshakeable faith convinced her that the phonetic Bible project was her divine calling. Armed with an iron will and limitless faith, she dedicated herself to this mission. Meanwhile, Christiana, full of eagerness to help with the project, was just about to make her mark when a sudden and unexpected change shifted the direction of her life.

FAITH IN THE DARKNESS: CHRISTIANA TSAI'S MIRACULOUS JOURNEY TO RECOVERY

In 1931, Christiana Tsai was struck by a severe case of malignant malaria that infiltrated her bone marrow, rendering her immobile for 17 days, speechless for eight months, and unable to open her eyes for a year and a half. Her prognosis was dire; the visiting Chinese doctor predicted she would not survive beyond three days. However, Miss Leaman, steadfast in her hope, sent cables around the world requesting prayers for Christiana's recovery.

While Christiana's family prepared for the worst, arranging for a coffin and grave clothes downstairs, Miss Leaman displayed her unyielding faith differently. She prayed fervently by Christiana's bedside and, in an act of defiance against despair, hired a tailor to make summer clothes for Christiana upstairs.

At the brink of death, Christiana experienced a vivid vision of a beautiful crown being lifted toward Heaven; she heard wonderful singing, and she thought to herself, "What a welcome!" But she heard a voice saying, "No, not a welcome, only practice." Awakening to find Miss Leaman praying and weeping beside her, Christiana began her slow journey to recovery.

However, recovery meant isolation in a darkened room, shielded from light and sound. The malaria destroyed her inner ear, robbing her of balance and causing dizziness with any movement, confining her to lying or sitting down. It also affected her eyes, necessitating glasses whenever the lights were on. Yet, she miraculously retained her vision and mobility, though this challenge tested her resilience greatly.

Throughout this challenging period, Miss Leaman lived with Christiana and was a steadfast pillar of support for her. By day, she tenderly cared for her, and by night, she poured her energy into the phonetic Bible project, tirelessly advancing their shared mission. Miss Leaman's dual dedication—to both Christiana's recovery and the groundbreaking project—demonstrated her unwavering commitment and resilience.

RESILIENCE AND FAITH: THE TRIALS AND TRIUMPHS OF MISS LEAMAN AND CHRISTIANA IN WARTIME CHINA

In 1937, as Miss Leaman was making significant strides with her phonetic Bible project, the Japanese invasion of China reached Nanking, forcing them to flee to the Shanghai concessions.[6] Amid the chaos of their hasty departure, there was no time for personal packing. Prioritizing her mission over personal belongings, Miss Leaman instructed her servant to pack all the phonetic Bible materials instead of her own clothes. Upon arriving in Shanghai, she found herself without a change of clothing and had to borrow garments from her servant.

Determined to complete her project, Miss Leaman chose to stay behind when other missionaries were repatriating. Her dedication was so intense that she nearly lost her eyesight finishing the last chapter of Revelation. By the time she completed the project, it was too late for her to catch the last evacuation ship to America.

After the 1941 attack on Pearl Harbor, Japanese forces took control of the Shanghai concessions, significantly tightening restrictions on foreign nationals. Labeled as "belligerent aliens"—a term the Japanese used for citizens from enemy countries—Miss Leaman and other Americans experienced curtailed freedoms. They were allowed limited movement within the city but were barred from leaving on the first exchange ship to America in June 1942.

---

6 The Shanghai concessions were areas of the city controlled by foreign countries, including Britain and France, from the mid-19th to the mid-20th centuries. These foreign powers governed the concessions with their own laws and police forces. This arrangement was established through treaties after China's defeats in conflicts like the Opium Wars.

By 1943, the situation deteriorated further as the Japanese set up concentration camps for these "belligerent aliens." However, those who were elderly or ill, like Miss Leaman, who suffered from a spinal condition, were temporarily spared, granted an extra year of grace before their inevitable internment.

In June 1944, as Miss Leaman prepared to enter the concentration camp following a Japanese summons, a continuous flow of visitors—40 to 50 a day—arrived to offer their sympathies during her final days of freedom. Despite her frail health, Miss Leaman greeted each guest with warmth, her unwavering composure and emotional resilience leaving a lasting impression. Remarkably, her strength in the face of adversity inspired a devoted Buddhist to embrace Christianity.

Miss Leaman was sent to a concentration camp on Lincoln Road, where approximately 250 elderly and sick prisoners were held for fourteen months without medical staff or supplies. The internees, some arriving on stretchers or leaning on crutches, others suffering from open wounds or blindness, faced grim conditions. They were housed in undiscriminating dormitories; within just three days, three had died, with many more to follow. However, their survival was aided by 50 young volunteers from other camps who cared for them and managed the arduous tasks.

Within the camp, Miss Leaman spent her days performing menial tasks such as peeling potatoes and cleaning moldy, dirty rice—their main sustenance. The daily meals consisted of this rice, swept from the floor and riddled with dirt, cooked with vegetable peelings in a large pot. Inmates lined up with buckets to receive this meager fare.

Even in these harsh conditions, Miss Leaman found ways to extend kindness, sharing the best portions of the food parcels she received from Christiana with fellow prisoners in dire need. Some of these prisoners, unable to consume the regular camp food due to diabetes, depended almost entirely on the sustenance she provided.

Throughout her fourteen-month ordeal, Miss Leaman battled dysentery and malaria, losing forty pounds and five inches in height due to her worsening spinal curvature. Yet, her spirit remained unbroken, and she continued to offer hope and support to those around her in even the darkest times.

After Miss Leaman was taken to a Japanese concentration camp, Christiana found herself alone, penniless, and without help as all their servants had departed. She rented a small attic room in an old house, keeping it dark due to her sensitivity to light. Unable to walk, Christiana had to crawl across the floor to move.

A neighboring Christian teacher kindly provided a warm meal each evening, while during the day, Christiana subsisted on hard biscuits and salted vegetables. In her moments of despair, she said to the Lord, "The way is too narrow, I cannot pass through." But God always answered her, "Hide in me, and I will take you through."

In a time of need, Christiana found support through an unconventional arrangement with her friend, Mrs. Temple. They struck a "Buddhist bargain": Mrs. Temple would assist Christiana in this life, and in return, Christiana would aid her in the next life. This pact brought Mrs. Temple into Christiana's dimly lit room regularly, where she not only helped with cooking but also provided much-needed companionship. Together in the dim room, while Mrs. Temple counted her prayer beads, they would sing hymns, read the Bible, and pray. By the year's end, both Mrs. Temple and her daughter had embraced Christianity.

However, Christiana's challenges intensified. Friends abroad who had promised monthly care packages for Miss Leaman could no longer afford to send them. With only two small cans of fruit and some charcoal left, Christiana faced a severe food shortage. As bank accounts were frozen, she resorted to selling her possessions and borrowing money at high interest rates to buy essential supplies like wheat biscuits, dates, and peanut butter to sustain Miss Leaman in captivity.

Rumors swirled that the Japanese were deliberately starving the internees. One morning, Christiana earnestly prayed for a five-pound tin of powdered milk for Miss Leaman. Just hours later, she received a surprising message: Brother Willow, a wealthy merchant, had felt convicted at Sunday service when the preacher declared that withholding tithes or failing to aid the needy was akin to robbing God. Moved by these words, Brother Willow decided to donate one of his three hoarded tins of powdered milk to Christiana for Miss Leaman.

Christiana was overwhelmed with relief and gratitude for this timely provision, which was impossible to purchase at any price. This divine intervention not only bolstered her faith but also proved crucial in sustaining Miss Leaman and others in the camp. Despite the lifesaving impact of these packages, the cost of sending them plunged Christiana into a debt of three thousand dollars.

ENDURING FAITH: CHRISTIANA AND MISS LEAMAN'S TRIUMPH OVER ADVERSITY

In August 1945, after eight long years of war, Japan surrendered. Christiana, traveling by rickshaw to the prison to see Miss Leaman, was stunned by her friend's frail and diminished appearance. Miss Leaman explained that American authorities had ordered her to remain in the camp for a month to prepare for immediate repatriation due to her health; doctors warned that any lifting or jolting could break her fragile spine.

Back home, Christiana was overwhelmed by a barrage of phone calls well into the night, and the next day brought no relief. By the third day, exhaustion took its toll; she began trembling uncontrollably and eventually fell unconscious, remaining in that state for four months.

Upon learning of Christiana's dire condition, Miss Leaman, driven by determination, sought permission from the American consulate to leave the camp and tend to her friend. Her initial request was denied due to her precarious health. Undeterred, Miss Leaman confronted the consul directly, spending the entire day sitting in his office until he, out of frustration, granted her three months' leave.

Despite her nearly broken spine, Miss Leaman made the grueling one-mile trek to Christiana's home, a remarkable feat given her fragile condition. Upon arriving, she found Christiana feverish and delirious, so much so that she didn't recognize Miss Leaman and called her "Big Brother."

In the midst of these hardships, both women faced significant financial challenges—Miss Leaman was penniless, and Christiana was encumbered with three thousand dollars of debt. Despite these adversities, their deep bond, strengthened by shared faith and love, kept their lives profoundly connected.

While Christiana lay unconscious, a man she had met only twice visited her. Upon hearing of her dire condition from Miss Leaman, he handed over a package, insisting, "I don't need this now. Use it and repay it when convenient." When Miss Leaman asked for his name and if he wanted a receipt, he simply replied, "Miss Tsai knows me, and I trust her. She is a Christian." Then he left. Inside the package, Miss Leaman discovered $3,100 in US currency!

With this unexpected windfall, they were able to rehire their servants, purchase medicine and food, seek medical advice for Christiana, and even pay off some of their debts.

Despite these efforts, Christiana's condition remained critical, her fever soaring as she teetered on the brink of death. The doctors who examined her offered little hope, revealing that her blood was infected with three of the most severe strains of malaria, with the parasites rapidly multiplying within her.

At the time, malaria was rampant in China and no cure was available locally. Miss Leaman learned from a doctor friend in America about an effective new malaria treatment, but it was not yet available in China. She was given a phone number, unattached to any name or address.

All of sudden, Miss Leaman remembered that a Chinese gentleman had come to her when she was entering prison, giving her his name, address, and phone number. He asked her to write to him if she got to America because he wanted to go to America. Afraid the Japanese would get hold of it, Miss Leaman tore it up and hid the pieces among the pages of her Bible. The Lord helped her to retrieve the pieces and put them together. She found out that he was the exact person who may have access to this medicine!

Contacting him, she learned his friend had just returned from America with 1,000 malaria pills intended for sale. Although the prescription stated it only took ten pills for a cure, Miss Leaman was offered the whole bottle for $350, take it or leave it!

After praying, Miss Leaman bought the whole bottle. Miss Leaman administered the medicine to Christiana, who was feverish at 106 degrees Fahrenheit, barely conscious, and unable to eat or move. She carefully fed Christiana three pills daily until the entire bottle was exhausted. Miraculously, Christiana's fever subsided, and she gradually regained consciousness. That was an unbelievable dose for any human body to absorb, let alone her tiny and frail one.

It took many months, but Christiana was finally brought back from the grave by God through Miss Leaman's unfailing love and tender care. Christiana's atheist doctor told Christiana later on, "Did you know that your family had been summoned to your deathbed and cried over you? In such a condition you were, and you are still here! I told my atheist family that my son and I had decided to follow the loving God."

Miss Leaman wrote to her family in August of 1947:

> I can hardly believe it is true, but day by day we watch Christiana coming back to life and strength! We bow our heads in wonder and thanksgiving for all that God has done. As the terrible pain and the indescribable suffering have lessened and flesh has come on her bones once again, and her movement becomes free, we realize that the Lord has wonderfully preserved her in body, mind, and spirit through so many years. These terrible malaria germs in her bones, which bound her in weakness, are diminishing and, as they decrease, she

> gains. The Lord in His great loving kindness and mercy seems to be restoring to her "the years that the locust hath eaten (Joel 2:25)."

BOUND BY FAITH: THE RESILIENT JOURNEY FROM CHINA TO AMERICA

As World War II came to an end, the Chinese Civil War reignited. The Communist forces steadily gained control of major cities and moved to expel foreign influences. Consequently, most missionaries fled China during this time. But Miss Leaman repeatedly booked and then canceled her passage to America, unwilling to leave Christiana in her fragile state.

Christiana told Miss Leaman, "But you go. Remember how the Japanese put you in the concentration camp. It may happen again with the changing government – or worse. I am Chinese. Somehow, I will be all right."

"No!" Miss Leaman said firmly. "I will die here with you if necessary!"

Recognizing the grave risks to Miss Leaman's safety in China, Christiana desired to accompany her to the United States. Yet Christiana had dwelled in darkness for eighteen long years, without light or sound. How could she endure a month's journey on a ship, sailing halfway around the world? How could she leave behind her beloved family and friends in China to venture into an unknown land like America? In her uncertainty, she prayed fervently.

Then, on three successive nights, the Lord spoke to her, saying, "Daughter, thy faith hath saved thee; go in peace." With her heart deeply rooted in faith, Christiana told Miss Leaman that the Lord had commanded her to go to the United States. So, she resolved to accompany her, despite the fear that she might not survive the long ocean voyage without adequate medical care and assistance.

At the American consulate, where Christiana applied for her visa, she faced another hurdle: a doctor required the removal of two fungus-infected fingernails to prevent the spread of infection. The painful procedure was carried out at her home by a doctor friend, but her finger got infected so badly that it went up into her arm about five inches and part of her arm needed to be amputated!

In a desperate attempt to control the infection, a second surgery was performed in her room. Miss Leaman was in tears praying for God's help during the second surgery. God once again answered her prayer. With a successful second surgery and by dipping her finger in medical waters day and night, Christiana's fingernail infection receded.

After weeks of recovery, just as Christiana's condition stabilized, they learned that only one last steamship was scheduled to depart China for the US. They were just in time to secure passage on this final vessel, ready at last to face the journey together.

When Miss Leaman contacted the steamship manager, she was disheartened to learn that 300 people were on the waiting list and their chances of boarding were slim. Nevertheless, she and Christiana prayed for a way.

In response to their prayers, a surprising call came from the manager: "Miss Leaman, two passengers fell ill and can't make the journey. I feel that I should let you two sick people have the first chance, and I'm going to bypass the waiting list. There are maybe six people in your cabin, however."

"Because we are sick, we don't want to bother others. If you could get a cabin for two, we would be grateful." Miss Leaman said. "I'll pray, as you try your best."

"Impossible, impossible," muttered the manager.

Then the Lord worked another miracle, and they had a cabin to themselves!

On January 19, 1949, Christiana was carried onto the ship by three doctors. Amid tearful farewells, she and Miss Leaman waved goodbye to family and friends, aware they might never meet again in this life.

Many of those who saw them off were later imprisoned and passed away, steadfast in their faith until the end.

At the ages of 59 and 69, Christiana and Miss Leaman, both in frail health, were carefully preserved by the Lord. Most people presumed that they would quietly fade away, including themselves, but the Lord had a different plan for them in the US.

FAITH'S BEACON: THE 35-YEAR MINISTRY OF CHRISTIANA TSAI AND MARY LEAMAN AT LEAMAN PLACE

Despite numerous hardships on their long journey, Miss Leaman and Christiana Tsai finally arrived at Leaman Place in Paradise, PA. Miss Leaman's sister Lucy and their cousin Mary W. Leaman eagerly awaited their arrival, filled with joy.

Due to Christiana's malaria, she was sensitive to light and sound. Her room had to be dark, with black curtains and wrapped light bulbs. In this confined space, only 12 feet wide and 15 feet long, Christiana prayed, "Lord, how can I serve You here, so far from the world's bustle?"

Even in her pain and illness, Christiana vowed to serve the Lord as long as she lived. Both she and Miss Leaman had dedicated their lives to spreading the gospel in China. Yet now, in the quiet of Leaman Place, they felt like fish out of water, longing to continue their ministry.

Their historic home, positioned by the busy Lincoln Highway, Route 30, was once an inn where horseback riders stopped to rest. Now, heavy traffic roared past day and night, while trains thundered along the nearby Pennsylvania Railroad. Despite this, the women sought ways to serve. They put up a bilingual sign on their front lawn that read, "Jesus Saves 信耶稣得救," which became a unique landmark. They opened their doors, ministering to everyone who came to visit.

Miss Leaman, also known as China Mary to distinguish her from her cousin Mary W. Leaman, served as the spiritual leader and managed the household. The four elderly women lived by a code: never criticize one another, never question motives, and never turn away an opportunity to witness for the Lord. They faithfully served together as a "harmonious quartet" with one mind and one spirit. While Christiana met visitors in her dark room, the other three ladies prayed in another room. Their harmony and faithfulness were evident, and God blessed their united spirit by bringing many guests to their door.

Figure 36: Christiana Tsai in the dark room.

Christiana, confined to her dark room, ministered to all who visited. This small space served as her office, dining room, reception area, and bedroom. Despite her pain and sleepless nights, she was determined to serve the Lord. She prepared each day, even through tears, trusting God to bring those in need to her.

Christiana Tsai was known for her famous saying during her testimonies: "I never, never ask God why; I only ask God what—Lord, what do you want me to do?" This message was particularly encouraging to those enduring their own pain and suffering, as it exemplified a simple yet profound faith in God.

Visitors brought in by Miss Leaman would sit on a small wooden chair from the Ming Deh Girls' School in Nanking. Among them were Rev. Ted and Leona Choy and Rev. Moses Chow, whose visits seemed divinely orchestrated. It was there, in 1956, that Rev. Ted and Leona first met Rev. Moses Chow. They later became special friends, co-founding AFC in 1963. In that dark room, the presence of God was palpable, offering solace and guidance to many through their ministry.

Their days were filled with visitors, whom they welcomed with open arms. Each morning, they prayed, "Lord, bring only those You desire, and keep away those who would drain our strength."

China Mary often spoke of cultivating "restful availability," a state where she remained at peace while open to receiving whoever God brought her way. Frequently, unexpected guests would arrive, and she welcomed them with the belief that each visitor was part of God's perfect plan.

After visiting Miss Tsai, visitors would often find themselves drawn to the humble abode of China Mary. With a warm smile, she would welcome them to join in singing her beloved hymn, "What a Friend We Have in Jesus." The lyrics, which spoke of the profound privilege of bringing all burdens to God in prayer, resonated deeply with everyone present. Through the simple yet powerful act of shared faith, China Mary's devotion to God shone brightly, uplifting the hearts of all who had the joy of being in her presence. Both China Mary and Christiana Tsai were known as women of deep and abiding prayer, their lives intertwined in a tapestry of faith and devotion.

Figure 37: Mary Leaman and Christiana Tsai.

In her solitary room, God called Christiana to write a book to witness for Him. "Lord, how can I write? And who would read it? I am nobody. Who knows my name?" Christiana questioned. She endured severe pain from recurrent malaria attacks, often unable to eat or sleep, lying in bed in relentless agony. The darkness of her room made it difficult to read or write.

Despite her poor health and doubts, Christiana kept God's calling in her heart and began jotting down outlines in a notebook whenever she was in less pain.

Two years later, Miss Ellen Drummond, another missionary descendant, came to visit them. They were old friends who had lived together in Shanghai for two years during wartime in China. When Christiana told her about the book project, Miss Drummond offered to help.

After endless praying and editing with a few Christian helpers, *Queen of the Dark Chamber* was published by Moody Press in 1953. The book was a huge success, reprinted 36 times in English from 1953 to 1976 and translated into over 30 languages, including Braille and film. This led to numerous conversions and baptisms, further spreading the gospel's reach.

Enthusiastic reviews and fan mail transformed their lives, bringing renewed interest and countless friends. Their driveway was soon filled with visitors from all over the world. They prayed daily, "May the Lord suggest, direct, and control all we say and do for Him and His children." On average, 43 guests visited daily for a period of time, keeping China Mary busy from morning till night. Additional help came as more people joined their ministry.

Though shy by nature, Christiana overcame her fears to serve the Lord wholeheartedly. She took the Holy Spirit as her mentor and her visitors as her mission. Many visitors, including military officers or sailors from Taiwan and Chinese students, came to faith through their ministry.

Leona Choy became very close friends with Christiana and the Leaman sisters. Leona helped Christiana write her second book, *Christiana Tsai,* and her third book, *Jewels from the Queen of the Dark Chamber*, spending countless hours in the dark room, editing, and reading the manuscript to Christiana, and enjoying quality time with the Leaman sisters.

Figure 38: Christiana Tsai, Lucy, China Mary, Mary W. Leaman

When Miss Leaman had a medical emergency, Christiana called on Leona Choy, who lived 125 miles away in Silver Spring, Maryland. Leona's station wagon became their ambulance, transporting Miss Leaman, Christiana, and her nurse to the emergency room together. Christiana insisted on staying with Miss Leaman at all times, so she was admitted to the hospital along with her, her famous Queen of the Dark Chamber status gaining special permission. Christiana served as Miss Leaman's relative, signing all the paperwork and holding her hand tightly even after Miss Leaman had passed on to Heaven. They had been together for 58 years, closer than blood relatives. Leona, their most trusted friend, took them to the hospital and later brought Christiana home.

Mary W. Leaman was called to the Lord in 1964, followed by Lucy in 1968, and finally Miss Leaman in 1972. Every four years, one of them went home to the Lord, leaving Christiana to carry on alone. Christiana's heart was indescribably sad; she simply didn't want to live anymore even though she was being taken good care of.

When Christiana wanted to "close the shop," she asked God to take her to Heaven to be reunited with Miss Leaman, her lifelong companion. But the Lord gave Christiana a vision:

"Suddenly I saw a vast wilderness, with dark clouds overhead. A figure appeared, walking very fast toward a bottomless pit. I could not distinguish the features. Then I heard a voice calling three times, 'Christiana, stop that person!'"

Christiana woke from her vision and realized the Lord was calling her. There was still work for her to do. She bowed her head and prayed, "Lord, forgive me for what I said. I do not want to hurt Thy feelings with my self-pity nor turn against my dear godmother's wishes. Lord, help me follow Thy leading, whatsoever Thou wouldst have me do."

Obeying God's call, Christiana continued her ministry despite her advanced age, infirmity, weakness, and increasing limitations. She served faithfully for another 12 years until she was in the arms of the Lord on August 25, 1984, at the age of 94.

Miss Leaman and Christiana Tsai dedicated 35 years to ministry in Leaman Place. Their partnership, rooted in deep faith and shared resilience, brought spiritual nourishment to many. Christiana, with her profound personal struggles and health issues, brought empathy and powerful testimony to their work, enriching their ministry with her unique insights and experiences.

Miss Leaman, equipped with a missionary's zeal and lifelong commitment to service despite battling a chronic spinal condition, provided robust leadership and spiritual mentorship. Their home became a sanctuary for countless souls seeking guidance and support, becoming a focal point for prayer meetings, Bible studies, and community gatherings.

Their influence extended beyond local bounds through Christiana's writings, which shared her inspiring life story and the transformative power of faith. This dynamic duo's legacy is remembered as one of unyielding courage, service, and profound faith amidst adversity.

PART THREE:

OUR FAITH JOURNEY AND BOND WITH AFC'S LAST FOUNDER

Chapter 5

OUR FAITH JOURNEY

A HERITAGE OF COURAGE AND GRIT: MY FATHER'S FAMILY HISTORY

According to records preserved by the local archival institution, the Yan family's genealogy dates back to 1414. During the Qing dynasty, a branch of my ancestors journeyed from Shanxi to Henan, following the river's winding path until they discovered a tranquil haven within the Tai Hang Mountain range. They settled there, herding sheep and making paper from a special grass. The village was named after a shop built by the Cang River by Bang Yan, the tenth-generation ancestor of the Yan family. Through their entrepreneurship, creativity, and hard work, their humble huts gradually evolved into a meticulously designed and well-constructed residential complex.

Construction of the residential complex began in 1724 AD during Emperor Qianlong's reign and continued through the Jiaqing period. This grand estate, covering an impressive 50,000 square meters, is nestled on three sides by mountains and faces the Cang River, offering breathtaking scenery. It features 10 courtyards with gates, walls, streets, and yards, along with 23 four-sided courtyard houses containing 86 rooms. Each section of the wall had gates for entry and exit, and watchtowers on the back mountain provided vigilant protection, making Xiaodian River Village （小店河村） an impregnable fortress.

There is but one path to enter the village, winding through the valley. At this entrance stands a monument, a steadfast sentinel, recounting the village's rich history and welcoming all who arrive.

Figure 39: Aerial View of Xiaodian River Village

Recognized as one of China's first traditional villages, this hamlet was honored in 2000 as a key cultural relic preserved by the Chinese government. Today, it stands not only as a testament to history but also as a beloved destination for tourists seeking its timeless charm.

During the turbulent years of the Japanese invasion of China, my father, Yuhe Yan (阎毓禾, 1926-2016), a descendant of the Yan family, lived here with his father, Doubin Yan (阎多滨, 1893-1956), and his mother, Youdao Wang (王有道, 1890-1966). My father was the youngest of four siblings. He had one sister and two brothers (阎毓淑, 阎毓杰, 阎毓东).

Nestled in a remote mountain location, Xiaodian River Village became a sanctuary, offering safety and tranquility despite its lack of a school. This peaceful environment nurtured my father's self-discipline and resilience, skills that would serve him well throughout his life.

Amidst the chaos of the Japanese invasion during World War II, my father, then a teenager, left his comfortable home with his brothers (his sister was already married and lived separately) and embarked on a perilous journey, navigating around Japanese-occupied areas in pursuit of an education. Despite having no means of support, he displayed incredible courage and an unwavering willingness to endure hardships. His journey was arduous and fraught with suffering, but his determination never wavered.

Encouraged and assisted by his elder brothers, he gained admission to the National Central University in Nanjing, the premier university in China at the time. After graduating as one of the top two students to receive a scholarship, he moved to Tianjin to teach, where he met my mother.

A HERITAGE OF PERSEVERANCE AND COMPASSION: MY MOTHER'S FAMILY HISTORY

My mother, Qiaoying Yu (俞巧英, 1926-2020), hailed from the picturesque Gooseneck Village (鹅颈村), named for the winding curves of its river in Ningbo. Beside this tranquil river stands the revered Yu Family Ancestral Hall, a sanctuary preserving the family's genealogies, origins, and historical documents. The history and development of the Yu family, along with the names of significant ancestors, are elegantly etched on bamboo tablets that grace the hall's walls.

Figure 40: The Ancestor Hall of the Yu Family

The Yu family lineage dates back to 1105 AD. At the heart of the hall stands a majestic statue of General Yu Dayou (俞大猷, 1503–1579). Renowned for his valiant resistance against Japanese pirates, Yu Dayou was a formidable Ming Dynasty general, strategist, martial artist, and poet. His achievements surpassed those of General Qi Jiguang (戚继光, 1528–1588). As the saying goes, "Jiguang is like a tiger, Dayou is like a dragon."

One section of the tablets documents the historic split and relocation of the family as it grew, while another section is dedicated to the names of ancestors, detailing the ranks they achieved in the imperial examinations—a rigorous process used from 605-1905 to select government officials—and the official positions they held.

The bamboo tablet that caught my eye was inscribed with The Yu Family Principles:

Revere ancestors and honor parents,
Foster unity among siblings,
Uphold righteousness in the household,
Promote peace with neighbors,
Choose mentors and friends wisely,
Diligently engage in farming and study,
Advance in knowledge and uphold traditions,
Commit to acts of kindness and strive for excellence,
Be diligent and trustworthy,
Value simplicity and hard work,
Speak thoughtfully and act prudently,
Stay humble and support others,
Respect laws and follow regulations.

I can see how my mother and her family members whom I knew personally embodied these principles in their lives. My grandfather, Chunyan Yu (俞纯彦, 1889-1959) and my grandmother, Yumei Fang (方玉梅, 1888-1979), led a life of modest means, neither impoverished nor affluent. The family could afford to send only their son to school, leaving their two daughters without the means for tuition. However, my mother, the youngest and brightest, was resolute in her pursuit of education. Her determination and hard work earned her a place at the prestigious Shanghai Nanyang Middle School and a Shu Ping Scholarship[7] to cover her tuition.

Figure 41: Ellen's Mother in Middle School.

During the tumultuous war years, the Shu Ping Scholarship (1939-1949) supported 1,065 students, allowing them to continue their education despite financial difficulties that would have made paying tuition challenging. One of these recipients was my mother.

To maintain the prestigious Shu Ping Scholarship, my mother had to consistently achieve top ranks in her class. Despite the immense pressure at an elite school with affluent classmates, she worked tirelessly, holding the top position throughout her middle and high school years. Her academic excellence and kindness earned the respect of her peers, leading to lifelong friendships that endured into her nineties.

In 1949, my mother graduated from the Private Nantong College with a degree in textiles, following in the footsteps of her father and brother, who were also in the textile industry. Her brother, who had entered the textile industry early to support the family, became an invaluable right-hand man to the factory owner. When the owner decided to establish a new factory in Tianjin, he entrusted her brother with the task, prompting the entire family to move from Ningbo to Tianjin.

---

7 The Shu Ping Scholarship was established by Gu Qianlin (1909-1998) in honor of his father, Gu Shuping. Guided by his father's counsel to earn money righteously and give back to society, Gu Qianlin created the scholarship to support academically outstanding but financially disadvantaged middle and high school students, reflecting the principle, "Receive from society, give back to society."

After completing her studies, my mother reunited with her family in Tianjin and began her teaching career in Tianjin University. It was there that she met my father.

Their connection quickly blossomed into a deep love, leading to their marriage on February 7, 1953. This marked the start of a beautiful 63-year journey together, rooted in love and shared purpose. Through life's ups and downs, they navigated with determination and trust, building a legacy of unwavering commitment and companionship.

Figure 42: Ellen's parents in 1953.

NAVIGATING TURMOIL: RESILIENCE DURING THE CULTURAL REVOLUTION

Born in 1964, I am the youngest of all my cousins on both sides of the family. During the Great Proletarian Cultural Revolution, I spent several years in the care of my uncle, Ansi Yu (俞安思, 1916–1972), and his wife, Qing Wang (王琴, 1918–2016). I also lived for a time with my aunt, Guiying Yu (俞媯英, 1922–2019), and my grandmother. They shielded me from the hardships my parents endured, treating me as their own, and I never felt homesick despite my parents' absence.

My grandmother, despite her bound feet and illiteracy—traits of her generation—was the kindest soul I have ever known, always showering love on everyone around her. My uncle's wife was very capable and wise, creating a warm and nurturing home where all my maternal cousins, including I, were raised for periods of time. She and I shared a mother-daughter bond. Even at age 98, she cooked for me when I visited. She passed away peacefully at age 99, without any illness.

The full impact of the Cultural Revolution was something I only came to understand much later in life, as I was just two years old when it began.

During the Cultural Revolution, society was starkly divided into the revolutionary "Red Five Categories (红五类)" and the persecuted "Nine Black Categories (黑九类)." The Red Five included revolutionary cadres, revolutionary soldiers, workers, poor peasants, and lower-middle peasants—groups considered loyal to the Party and, as a result, granted protection.

In stark contrast, the Nine Black Categories were branded as enemies of the revolution. These included landlords, rich peasants, counter-revolutionaries, bad elements (坏分子), rightists (右派), traitors (叛徒), spies (特务), capitalist roaders (走资派), and intellectuals—the latter scornfully labeled as the "Stinking Old Ninth (臭老九)."

Intellectuals faced severe persecution and public humiliation, and were often sent to labor camps for "reeducation," disrupting education and scientific research. My parents, both college professors, belonged to the "Stinking Old Ninth" and endured brutal treatment.

My father was confined to a "cowshed," separated from my mother, and detained in makeshift prisons with rudimentary facilities. He was forced to document every detail of his life while enduring physical abuse and public shaming through "big-character posters"—large handwritten signs criticizing and denouncing individuals, prominently displayed in the university bulletin area where he worked.

In a cowshed, my father was forced to write countless documents to the Chinese Communist Party (CCP), proclaiming his support for the revolution. Many years later, these handwritten materials were returned to him, and before he passed away, he entrusted them to me. These poignant writings spoke volumes about his perseverance and endurance. While many of his colleagues succumbed to suicide during these relentless attacks, my father, with nerves of steel and a will of iron, endured.

My mother, his true soulmate, stood by him and supported him unwaveringly, regardless of the accusations my father faced. She trusted in his innocence and honesty, always knowing his intentions were good. Many families were torn apart, as the CCP induced loved ones to "set up boundaries," leaving those under attack vulnerable and fragile. But not my mother. She remained steadfast beside my father despite the relentless attacks and humiliations. Neither my father nor my mother joined the Communist Party, which may explain why they were treated so brutally during the Cultural Revolution.

In 1970, my parents were sent to the countryside for "reeducation," compelled to endure hard labor and farming. My grandmother, my sister, and I followed, staying there for three years. I was only six years old when we began this arduous journey into rural life and farming.

Despite the harsh conditions that severely impacted my parents' health, my father instilled in me the importance of courage, critical thinking, and perseverance—values his own father had imparted to him during wartime. My mother, embodying the industriousness, resilience, and compassion that the Yu family had instilled in her, taught me to uphold these virtues even in the toughest environments. These inherited family values and virtues guided me through the most challenging times of my life's journey.

In 1976, the death of Mao Zedong, the founding father of the People's Republic of China, and the reinstatement of college entrance exams by Vice Premier Deng Xiaoping marked the end of the Cultural Revolution. This pivotal shift refocused the nation on education, opening a new chapter in our lives and in the future of China.

A JOURNEY OF FAITH AND RESILIENCE

In 1979, I was accepted into Tianjin Nankai Middle School, a prestigious institution founded in 1904 by Yan Xiu and known for its illustrious alumni, including Premiers Zhou Enlai and Wen Jiabao. Following my parents' example of industriousness and self-discipline,

Figure 43: Ellen in 1986.

I graduated with top scores in the national college entrance examination. This led me to pursue undergraduate studies at the People's University of China and graduate studies at Nankai University. The strong values and rigorous training instilled at home and school laid a solid foundation for my future endeavors.

In 1987, I received the prestigious Sino-American Economic Exchange Program scholarship, funded by the Ford Foundation. This enabled me to study economics for a year in Beijing under top American professors with American textbooks. Their strong recommendations helped me secure admission and a full assistantship to the University of Iowa.

Figure 44: Bing, Ellen, and Reece in 1995.

On August 16, 1988, with only $40 in my pocket and a singular ambition to earn my Ph.D. in economics, I embarked on a journey from China to the United States.

In 1989, I married my husband, Bing Liang. Our joy multiplied in 1991 with the birth of our son, Reece, marking the beginning of a new chapter in our journey.

My first ten years in the US were consumed by intense academic and career pursuits. Immersed in heavy coursework, research, and raising a child, I had little time or inclination to consider spiritual messages. Having never been exposed to religion and with no family history of faith, spirituality remained a distant concept in my busy life.

Figure 45: Ellen at KeyCorp in 1999.

It wasn't until I had firmly established my career and family life that I felt a profound longing, realizing that professional success couldn't satisfy the deeper desires of my soul. This awakening led me to seek solace and fulfillment in the spiritual realm.

In 1999, as regular church visits became part of our family routine, our pastor delivered a prophecy that would profoundly shape our lives: "God will bless you with a daughter." At that time, our family felt complete—my husband Bing, an aspiring finance professor at Case Western University, our eight-year-old son Reece, and myself, a vice president of risk management at KeyCorp, a commercial bank. Expanding our family hadn't crossed our minds, yet this prophecy hinted at an unforeseen future.

As I reflect on my initial journey into motherhood, it unfolded under the weight of challenges, particularly as a Ph.D. student. My husband and I, deeply immersed in our doctoral studies, welcomed our son into our modest graduate student life. Financial constraints compelled us to seek support from my mother-in-law, who traveled from China to help us through this new chapter. With three generations living under one roof during this time, we struggled. Personal losses in our extended families back in China cast a shadow of grief over our days, amplifying our absence of faith.

Despite these challenges, graduating and starting our professional careers significantly improved our lives. However, the lingering echoes of those tumultuous times cast shadows on our family dynamics, especially with our busy dual-career lifestyle. In search of understanding and support, we turned to faith for guidance and reconciliation.

In 1999, Pastor Che Ann from Korea visited Cleveland, Ohio. During his sermon, our son Reece, moved by the Holy Spirit, embraced Christianity, marking a profound beginning for our family. He was the first to respond to the Lord's call, while Bing and I stood at a crossroads.

In the days that followed, driven by a deep longing to encounter the Almighty, I embraced regular worship, seeking God's unmistakable presence. My soul yearned for experiences that would strengthen my faith and anchor my trust in the promise that God was actively moving in our lives.

In late 1999, facing minor surgery a week before a key business conference in London, I turned to prayer, entrusting my health to God. Miraculously, the trip went smoothly, enriching me with invaluable connections and experiences, and deepening my commitment to Christ.

At a Thanksgiving Christian Conference in Chicago in 2000, Pastor Che Ann's Holy Spirit-infused sermon profoundly touched Bing's heart, leading him to embrace Jesus as his Savior. On November 26, 2000, a significant chapter in our spiritual journey unfolded as our family was baptized by Rev. Joseph Tai in a Hyatt Hotel hot tub. This transformative event marked a distinct point in our spiritual journey. Four months later, the birth of our daughter, Mina, joyously confirmed God's blessings and the truth of His promise and grace.

When my family embraced baptism and entered the fellowship of Christianity, our journey with God became both challenging and exhilarating, filled with joyous revelations and unexpected paths. Through experiences marked by trials and triumphs, we learned the essence of walking by faith—a journey not just toward God, but with God, at every turn and twist of life's path.

A PROPHECY ABOUT OUR RELOCATION

At the Christian Thanksgiving Conference in Chicago in 2002, I was among a group of devout Christians, all of us eager to hear from Pastor Ye of Taiwan, a speaker known for his prophetic gifts. Our paths had never crossed before, yet it seemed our meeting was destined. Even though many years have passed, that conversation remains vividly etched in my memory, as if it happened only yesterday.

Figure 46: Bing, Reece, and Ellen got baptized In 2000.

As my turn approached for the pastor to pray for me amongst the line of other eager Christians, I stepped forward, my heart heavy with uncertainty, explaining our family's relocation dilemma without a seemingly clear destination. Pastor Ye paused, closed his eyes in a brief prayer, and then, with piercing clarity, asked, "Is there a place on the East Coast you've considered, one you've sought God's guidance on?" I could only nod in affirmation. "God said you may go to that place," he proclaimed. In response to my anxious question, "When?" he answered with unwavering certainty, "Next spring." His words cut through my doubt with absolute clarity. As he turned to address the next person in line, I was left in a quiet cocoon of contemplation, reflecting on the profound simplicity of his guidance.

In the spring of 2003, a refreshing breeze of change swept through our lives. Bing received an invitation to present his research at a seminar at the University of Massachusetts, Amherst, close to Boston—the city we had long prayed over. Although the presentation was not part of a traditional job market, his expertise in hedge funds aligned seamlessly with the business school's newly established Hedge Fund Center. Remarkably, despite a stringent budget freeze, the school was able to secure a position, which received approval at every necessary level. It seemed divinely orchestrated that he should move there.

Amherst, with its quaint university charm about 90 miles west of Boston, offered no straightforward path for my career in quantitative risk management, where my expertise lay. The thought of moving there was daunting to me, yet in the serene sanctuary of reflection, I recalled the place for which we had prayed. The opportunity's alignment with the prophetic guidance we had received was undeniable, compelling me to see it as God's will, and prompting me to set aside my reservations in submission to a greater plan.

A DIVINE INTERVENTION: DREAMS, VISIONS, AND DECISIONS

By the summer of 2003, we had settled in Amherst, where Bing's career flourished. He progressed from associate professor to full professor and eventually to chair professor, earning numerous accolades, including teaching awards and a prestigious research and innovation award from his university. His achievements established him as a globally recognized scholar, fulfilling the prophetic words of Aunty Mei Lian, a revered servant of God with the gift of prophecy and sister of Rev. Joseph Tai, who baptized us. Even before our daughter was born, she had predicted that Bing would one day become a world-renowned scholar and an important co-worker in God's kingdom.

Figure 47: Ellen, Bing, Mina, and Reece in 2003.

Moving to Amherst, a remote university town, marked a dramatic shift for me. Suddenly, my rising career trajectory had come to an indefinite pause, a dynamic that Aunty Mei Lian had previously foreseen. When she first prophesied this, I was incredulous. Fresh from earning my Ph.D. in financial economics and serving as a vice president of Risk Management at a commercial bank, my professional future seemed luminous. The prospect of becoming a stay-at-home mother instead of the successful career woman I aimed to be was unimaginable.

Yet, through these trials, the narrative of our lives continued to weave a tapestry of divine orchestration, reminding us that our paths often have deeper intentions than we might initially perceive. It became clear that obedience to God's direction is crucial, lest we, like Jonah in the Bible, face great challenges for straying from our intended course.

After we moved to Amherst, advancing my career became immensely challenging. Despite my strong educational background and strong corporate experience, the town's remote location limited my job opportunities. Restlessness set in, and I began exploring positions in larger cities, though they were too far for daily commuting. Eventually, I was prepared to sacrifice some family time to preserve my professional and emotional well-being.

Soon, an excellent opportunity emerged—a job offer from a Boston consulting firm where I connected deeply with the hiring manager, a Chinese woman. We developed a rapport that almost bordered on friendship during my interview. Understanding my family commitments, she offered a flexible arrangement allowing me to work from home two days a week. The role involved research and analysis, areas I was both trained in and passionate about. However, the job was 90 miles from home, a significant concern given that our children were just three and 12 years old. The idea of daily commuting was unfeasible. I found myself wondering, why couldn't we find a midpoint for our home, perhaps in a city like Worcester? Tired of being confined at home, I was determined not to let the opportunity slip away.

Figure 48: Ellen with her parents and Reece in 1995.

I proposed staying in Boston three days a week and working from home the remaining two, ready to make this sacrifice for my cherished career. The high-pressure environment was something I thrived in, and staying home had become increasingly difficult. The company, keenly interested, extended the offer repeatedly over two months. However, accepting the job would strain our family life, affect my involvement in raising our children, and commit me to navigating Boston's notorious traffic. It felt like a desperate attempt to stay afloat.

At a moment of great indecision, I had a vivid dream that left an indelible mark on me. In the dream, I approached a road and was terrified by a monstrous figure coming from the other direction. Frightened, I ran back to a small, lit house in a vast, wild field seeking refuge. I awoke with my heart racing and hands sweating, convinced that this was a divine vision advising me against the job, since I seldom dreamed.

As I lay in bed contemplating the vision, the phone's ring pierced the silence—an international call from my father in China. As distinguished college professors and renowned researchers, my parents raised my sister and me to believe in our limitless potential, challenging societal norms. Inspired by their ethos, my sister earned a Ph.D. in physics and I in financial economics, continuing their legacy in the US.

This call was extraordinary, given the high costs and logistical hurdles of early 2000s China. My father had to make a rare nighttime visit to a special post office to place the only call he ever initiated during our many years of trans-Pacific conversations. It was clearly of the utmost importance to him. He had learned of my job situation from my sister, and his unexpected advice was: as a mother, prioritize family over career!

His counsel left me speechless. He had always encouraged me to break through societal barriers that favored men, having raised only two daughters with the belief that we were just as capable as any man. That morning, when he advised me to prioritize family over my professional ambitions, I was genuinely stunned.

The convergence of the vision and my father's call struck me as divine signals. Overwhelmed and seeking direction, I knelt in prayer and ultimately chose to decline the job offer, surrendering to God's will.

In 2010, after more than ten years of sincere prayers for my parents, divine healing restored my mother's hearing, which she had lost for nearly a month. Following this miraculous event, both my parents accepted Christ and were baptized by Bing. Today, they rest peacefully in God's arms, laid to rest in Yan's ancestral burial ground in Xiaodian Village, Henan.

NAVIGATING NEW REALITIES AND DIVINE ASSIGNMENTS

Throughout my career struggles, God knew my frustrations. Later that year, a major corporation in Hartford discovered my resume online and offered me a research position that perfectly matched my skills. Despite the two-and-a-half-hour daily commute, I accepted the job, finding fulfillment in work that aligned with my training and passions.

In March 2007, we had the honor of hosting Mary Wang, the general director of the Chinese Overseas Christian Mission (COCM), and her husband Ernest from the United Kingdom (UK) during our pastor's ordination. They stayed with us for a few days while our children, Reece and Mina, were on a school break. One evening, we had a profound conversation that deeply influenced my life.

Mary, with a gentle demeanor and voice reminiscent of my mother, shared captivating stories from her past, including being a medical student trapped in China during the communist takeover while her family relocated to Hong Kong. That night, she introduced me to homeschooling through the story of Susanna Wesley, who educated her ten children at home, including John Wesley. John once remarked, "I learned more about Christianity from my mother than from all the theologians in England."

This was my first exposure to homeschooling. Mary observed, "Your two children are very special. If you raise them in a godly way and let God use them later, it will be a bigger contribution to society than your efforts as a working mom."

Inspired by Mary's insights, I prayed for guidance, feeling that God had spoken through her, suggesting that nurturing our children in a godly manner could be more impactful than my professional achievement.

Following Mary and Ernest's return to the UK, a series of family events prompted me to reassess my priorities. Despite the challenges we faced, it became clear that my family needed me more than my salary. Therefore, on June 6, 2007, I resigned from my cherished corporate job to fully embrace God's will, embarking on a challenging yet rewarding new journey.

Adapting to life at home proved immensely challenging for me. From my early years through education and career, I had been steeped in a culture of fierce competition. In China, maintaining a position at the top of my class had required not only intellect and dedication but also the willingness to sacrifice my personal life. This intense commitment had shaped my entire approach to living, so much so that when I found myself at home, I felt utterly out of place, like a fish out of water. Mood swings became frequent as I grappled with my new reality and often questioned my decision.

In moments of deep reflection, I would ask God, "Why should I set aside my hard-earned Ph.D., decades of elite education, and years of valuable corporate experience to stay home and care for our children? Isn't this a squandering of society's investment in me?" I cried out to God, struggling to understand why I couldn't be both a successful career woman and enjoy a fulfilling family life. Yet, in those moments of turmoil, God seemed silent. Then, I recalled a prophecy from Aunty Mei Lian many years ago, who had foretold that I would be a noble stay-at-home mother. It appeared that my path had been divinely chosen.

However, the stark contrast between my former life and my new reality was overwhelming. Alone at home, without the accolades and recognition I was accustomed to, I struggled with the realization that God's plan for me diverged sharply from my dreams. Yet, I came to understand the irreplaceable role of my presence in nurturing our children's spiritual, emotional, and physical growth. I realized that these responsibilities could not be effectively outsourced without negatively impacting our family dynamics and our children's fulfillment of God's intended purpose.

After months of wrestling with God in prayer, I found peace and began to cherish the precious family life I had been given. I dove into research on biblical parenting, applying my findings to our family life. As our son Reece approached the pivotal juncture of his 11th-grade year, embarking on the rigorous journey of college applications, our bond flourished through shared experiences like campus visits and heartfelt discussions. That same year, he was selected as one of only two boys to represent Massachusetts at Boys Nation in Washington D.C., an honor that profoundly influenced his later life.

Figure 49: Ellen, Reece, Bing, and Mina in 2010.

Our joint navigation through the college admissions process was a journey of discovery and depth. Armed with a passion for research and an array of comprehensive guides on college applications, I supported Reece with fervor and insight. This period was transformative; it deepened our connection, providing him with unwavering support during a crucial phase of his life. As the pressures of high school life mounted, my role as a vigilant parent became all the more essential—a role I could fully embrace only after stepping away from my corporate responsibilities.

Throughout this time, I was profoundly aware that I was not alone in guiding Reece. Bing strongly supported me. God, in His infinite wisdom, orchestrated Reece's path in remarkable ways. Reece pursued his undergraduate education at Swarthmore College, a place he dearly loved, graduating a semester early to embark on a successful career that spanned prestigious firms like Analysis Group and Goldman Sachs. Having completed his MBA at the London Business School, he ascended to the role of Technology Director at Jones Lang LaSalle, as a distinguished leader in the commercial real estate industry.

Despite facing significant challenges and periods of doubt in his faith, Reece's spiritual resilience grew, and his faith ultimately deepened and strengthened. The transformation in Reece's life was so profound that I could not help but praise God's abundant mercy and grace. His guiding hand was unmistakable. Blessed by the Lord, Reece not only achieved success in his professional life but also began to build a family of his own. On March 22, 2024, he married Lisa, a devoted sister in faith and a medical doctor who graduated from Harvard Medical School. Together, they have wholeheartedly committed themselves to their church in Boston, faithfully serving their ministry and the wider community. Reece also serves as the head of the visiting council at Williston Northampton School, a place he holds dear, where he served as class president throughout his high school years.

The intense involvement in my son's adolescent years and beyond underscored the critical role I played as a mother. Through my dedicated presence, guided by divine grace and profound familial love, I came to appreciate the enduring impact of our shared journey—a testament to the mysterious and loving ways in which God molds our lives.

THRIVING IN HOMESCHOOLING

In 2010, as our son began college and my husband Bing prepared for a sabbatical at Yale University, we planned to relocate to New Haven. However, we faced a regulatory hurdle with our daughter Mina's school, Pioneer Valley Chinese Immersion Charter School (PVCICS), which only allowed new admissions at specific grades to maintain consistent language proficiency. If Mina left for half a year, she would be considered a new student and ineligible to rejoin her class.

Despite explaining that our daughter, an exemplary student, would maintain her Chinese proficiency under my tutelage, the school remained firm on its policy. In our frustration, we recalled a congratulatory note from a Massachusetts senator to my husband and decided to seek his intervention. Unfortunately, despite his efforts, our appeal was rejected.

Distraught and unable to shake my anger for weeks, a piercing question from God halted my spiraling thoughts: "What if I am the One who closed all the doors for her to return to her school?" This startling notion led me to a quiet surrender, accepting that perhaps God intended for us to take a different path. Recalling prophetic words about Mina from our pastor, "She would use music to worship God," and from Aunty Mei Lian, "She is talented in music," I embraced the idea of homeschooling with renewed vigor and dedication.

Figure 50: Ellen began to homeschool Mina in 2010.

Thus began our new chapter at Harbor Close, a serene, gated community near Yale. Our home, perched above the ocean harbor, offered breathtaking views where swans glided under the golden morning sun. Evenings were often spent clam digging and catching crabs—a cherished pastime from Bing's childhood.

On our journey, we discovered the Massachusetts Homeschool Organization of Parent Educators (MASSHOPE), a vibrant community supporting Christian homeschool families in the state. Through their annual conferences, we were introduced to TeenPact Leadership School and the National Christian Forensics and Communications Association (NCFCA) Christian Speech & Debate League. These organizations offered our children invaluable leadership and debate opportunities, enriching their education and training throughout their homeschooling experience.

The homeschooling community was unfamiliar to Mina at first, but the genuine warmth and respect she encountered soon made her feel at home. As Mina excelled in debates, my involvement deepened; I learned to serve as a judge at tournaments. This exposure to the homeschooling world was enlightening, brimming with enriching experiences and deep insights into parenting.

Figure 51: Mina won top talent award in 2019.

I taught Mina math and Chinese, while she excelled in English, Latin, and violin with the help of skilled instructors. Her afternoons were filled with ballet, competitive swimming, and orchestra, contributing to a joyful and enriching homeschooling experience. Her talents blossomed, earning her recognition as a principal violinist and swimming champion at a young age.

Her deep faith, fostered through our family's spiritual journey, became a foundational pillar of her growth, continuing to sustain her well beyond her homeschooling days.

In 2015, Mina was admitted to Deerfield Academy, a distinguished boarding school in New England. There, she thrived, consistently making the honor roll, serving on the student council, and excelling as a varsity swimmer. In her later years of high school, she began participating in performing arts competitions, earning the title of Distinguished Young Woman (DYW) of Massachusetts in 2019. She represented the state at the national competition in Mobile, Alabama, where she earned a Top National Talent Award for her self-choreographed ballet and violin performance.

In May of 2024, Mina graduated from Columbia University and got an exceptional job offer from a prestigious boutique investment banking firm in New York City. In July of 2024, she won the first runner-up in the prestigious Miss New York competition.

On the candidate profile page of the 2024 *Miss New York* magazine, Mina was asked, "What is the one thing you can't live without?" Her response was: "My faith. I am blessed to have been raised in a Christian family, and I find courage in knowing that He holds me in His hands. I can love because I am loved so deeply, and I strive to extend hope to others because of the hope that has been given to me."

Figure 52: Reece and Mina served as hosts in 2024.

In 2023 and 2024, Reece and Mina had the privilege of serving as bilingual hosts for the Asian American Day Festival in Boston. I had the joy of crafting the Chinese scripts, while Bing served as a photographer.

The four of us share a deep passion for serving—both within our church and in the wider community. We find great joy in traveling and embracing new adventures together as a family. As we look ahead, we are preparing for a mission trip to Africa, where we will help establish a microloan program. Alongside a team of believers led by Pastor Jian Zhu, we seek to bring relief to the region, trusting that God will work through us to alleviate poverty and transform lives. Our prayer is that He will use us as vessels for His glory. May His hand guide each step we take, and may His love give us the strength and wisdom to serve the people He has placed before us.

Chapter 6

OUR SPIRITUAL KINSHIP WITH MRS. LEONA CHOY

THE DIVINE FAREWELL

In the wee hours of March 2, 2023, I composed a lengthy and enthusiastic email to Leona, detailing my thrilling journey to Wilmore, Kentucky, where I attended the Asbury Revival. I also asked if my family could visit her on May 14, Mother's Day, while we were in Pennsylvania commemorating the 60th anniversary of Ambassadors for Christ Inc. (AFC).

Figure 53: Mrs. Leona Choy

A few hours later, at 8:00 a.m., I received an email from her son Rick informing me that Leona's condition had taken a drastic turn for the worse, rendering her unconscious. He expressed his concerns that she might not make it through the day.

Later, we learned that Leona went home to the Lord at 9:30 a.m. that same day. The news was posted on her Facebook page, proclaiming that she had shed her "earthly suit" and returned to her Heavenly Father. I was devastated, and a deep sorrow washed over me as I pondered the profound journey of our relationship, which had grown and flourished under the watchful eyes of our God.

MRS. LEONA CHOY'S FAREWELL LETTER

Leona's pre-written farewell letter was posted on Facebook, conveying the following message:

> My Dear Friends and Family,
>
> I pray this message finds you all safe and healthy.
>
> I know that many of you have been concerned about me. I am honored and blessed that you would take the time to inquire about my lack of communication over the past few months.
>
> This past year has brought some health challenges and I now find myself really feeling my 97 years! As a result, I have been seeking the Lord for His direction regarding "retirement" of sorts. I believe He has spoken and I am ready to move on into the next phase of my "ordered days." I will no longer be able to produce my regular blog as I have for so many years due to fatigue of body and mind. This has been a difficult decision and only arrived at through much prayer and seeking God's will.
>
> I am very grateful for the many opportunities He has given me to minister to His people. I am very grateful, as well, for all of you and your faithfulness in following me on this journey.
>
> Resting in His will for me at this time,
>
> Leona

There will be a Celebration of Life for Leona Choy on Monday, March 13, 2023, at Omps Funeral Home, Amherst Chapel, 1600 Amherst St, Winchester, VA.

Despite having known her for only two years and meeting her in person just once, I felt a profound spiritual and personal bond with her. She became my spiritual mentor and American mother. Our friendship began in 2020 when I received a calling to write about the lives of missionaries.

A DIVINE CONNECTION: THE START OF A SPIRITUAL JOURNEY

In March 2021, with a hopeful spirit, I dialed the customer service number listed on the Ambassadors for Christ (AFC) website. To my delight, the voice on the other end extended far beyond the basic courtesies of an informational call. Not only did she offer to send me the biographies of their founders as I had requested, but she also informed me about their last surviving founder, Leona, and directed me to her personal website.

Compelled by this unexpected lead, I promptly reached out to Leona through her website and followed up with an email laden with my eagerness, including an introduction to my book, a chapter sample, and personal testimonies of my encounters with God. Leona's response was nothing short of warm personal greetings and comprehensive. Her email arrived on March 14, 2021, and included the following excerpts:

> Dear Ellen,
>
> I am delighted to make a new writing friend and eager to assist with your project. Your undertaking sounds intriguing. Who backs your project, and who are your readers? Given the subjects you're exploring, consider the audience's accessibility to similar material and the language barrier for readers in China.
>
> Presently, I am finalizing my memoir, Slow Boat to China, which reflects on my 73 years in Chinese ministries. This book might address many of your questions. I've also penned

> biographies available through AFC, and am seeking translators for some of my other works.
>
> Your connection to Iowa piqued my interest, and I would be glad to discuss more via phone or email. Despite my advanced years, my passion for writing and ministry burns as brightly as ever.
>
> Blessings,
>
> Leona

The bond with Leona formed swiftly and deeply, growing to possess an almost maternal quality. This connection became especially significant as I approached the first anniversary of my mother's passing on March 18, 2020. Due to Covid-related travel restrictions, I was unable to return to China for her memorial service, and my heart ached with her absence.

In this moment of profound sorrow, Leona's timely and thoughtful reply felt like a divine gift, providing solace and nurturing a new friendship amidst my grief. Leona, one year older than my mother, extended warmth and kindness that deeply moved me. With gratitude, I replied the following day:

> I am deeply touched by your response. Our connection feels divinely ordained, transcending our age difference through the shared spirit of God's words. Your vast experience and wisdom are invaluable to me as I navigate this project inspired by God's direction.
>
> This project is a leap of faith, much like when I felt called to homeschool my daughter. Although daunting, I've learned that such obedience is often met with profound blessings.
>
> Your prolific achievements and ongoing contributions at the age of 95 inspire me immensely. I would cherish an opportunity to introduce myself further through a video call or phone conversation.

Thank you for considering sharing your insights and possibly your books for my research. I look forward to potentially speaking with you soon.

Two days later, Leona replied with warmth, expressing delight in our growing friendship and the divine purpose it might fulfill.

I'm really so happy to get to know you, Ellen! **I feel that the Lord has some special purpose in our new friendship.**

I enjoyed your pictures on Facebook and getting to know about your lovely, handsome and gifted family. This is just a quick response to support you in your writing. You write well, and I believe with your research background and motivation you will be successful.

But let me digress...I personally think that your most significant and influential book could be written with your own story and experience and struggle which is so common among Chinese academic families, especially those studying in the US and then becoming professionals in their career—trying to raise families while maintaining careers. Especially in the Christian context.

Ellen, your story is SO COMPELLING! And you are such a good writer having lived out the struggle successfully with homeschooling. But your surrender to the Lord's will first. You are a role model of how it can be done with the Lord's help. Truly a success story on every front.

Actually, I see first your story in Chinese as a feature article in AMBASSADOR MAGAZINE as an appetizer and then expand it into book form. Perhaps AFC could be the publisher? I think you have a winning subject, so very relevant to all professional Chinese families. Write your book in Chinese or English, as you please. And include pictures.

Have you considered this before? I hope you could pray about this and see how the Lord would lead. I'm serious.

I really want to send you some books as my contribution to your research if you would give me your mailing address.

I attach a few pictures. I have 4 sons and 10 grandchildren and 13 great-grandchildren. My youngest grandson just enlisted in the Army. The first picture is my 90th birthday 6 years ago. The final is all 4 of my sons.

Figure 54: Leona with her four sons. Richard, Gary, Clifford, Jeffrey.

Leona's words of encouragement strengthened my determination to continue this writing project and deepen my spiritual walk with the Lord. As I carefully sifted through the autobiographies of the missionaries, I leaned on the guidance of the Holy Spirit to discern which stories to include and which to leave aside. This writing endeavor became a sacred journey, drawing me closer to God and enabling me to serve as an instrument of His will.

THE IOWA CONNECTION

Leona was born on June 22, 1925, in Cedar Rapids, Iowa, where she spent her early years. In 1947, she married Ted Choy in Cedar Rapids.

It is indeed a small world. Rev. Ted Choy, my husband Bing Liang, and I are all alumni of the University of Iowa. Rev. Choy earned his master's degree in theology in 1955, while Bing and I graduated from the College of Business in the mid-90s. By a charming twist of fate, our wedding dates nearly coincide: Ted and Leona married on August 23, 1947, and Bing and I on August 22, 1989, both during the intense heat of the Iowa summer.

During our initial correspondence, Leona fondly brought up our shared roots in Iowa. As Bing prepared to attend a reunion at the University of Iowa's College of Business in April 2022, we reached out to Leona, who graciously shared the address of her childhood home at Cedar Rapids, Iowa.

Figure 55: Leona's childhood house in Cedar Rapids, Iowa.

In her touching email, Leona wrote:

> Ellen, your note brought a flood of memories. Sadly, all from my parents' generation and most from my own, including relatives and classmates, have passed away. The last time I visited, just a few years ago, was on a road trip with my son Cliff. We stayed in a motel and managed to visit some of the remaining family friends, who are now all gone. It feels surreal that no one from my past is left in what was once my vibrant hometown.
>
> The house where I grew up, now repeatedly renovated and turned into a rental, still show up in my dreams. If Bing could snap a photo, it would mean so much to me, though I no longer know the current tenants.

Although Bing found the house unoccupied during his visit, he captured several photographs, which he later sent to Leona. She confirmed it was indeed her former residence and expressed her heartfelt gratitude for Bing's thoughtful gesture.

> Bing, thank you so much for the photos. It's astonishing—the mailbox we bought back in 1930 is still there! We never had a tree in our front yard, and everything looks much smaller than in my childhood memories.

These exchanges not only reconnected Leona with her past but also deepened our connection to her, illustrating the profound impact of place and memory in our lives.

FROM ACQUAINTANCE TO FAMILY

After I shared my address with Leona, her bountiful gifts of books began arriving weekly, each package containing three to four of her published books. Moved by her generosity, I contributed to her publishing ministry through her website, leonachoy.com, and our correspondence blossomed with tales of my family's daily endeavors.

My email to her was filled with appreciation:

> Your third parcel has just arrived, bringing another four treasures of your books! My daughter Mina, usually a whirlwind of energy, has found solace in your book 'This is your life—write it.' The pandemic has changed her world, yet your words encourage her budding passion for writing. Please take a moment to watch this video, in which she danced ballet while playing violin. Thank you so much for your passion in sending me all those wonderful books. We'd love to meet you on zoom when it is convenient for you.

Her reply warmed my heart:

> Mina is truly a gifted and versatile young lady! Watching her video was a delight; her talent in both ballet and violin is remarkable. Also, I was deeply touched by your generous donation to my publishing ministry—thank you for your profound kindness.
>
> While my operations are business-like, my heart lies in ministry, sharing books with those who cherish or need them, without any intent for profit. This endeavor is indeed a non-profit ministry dedicated to uplifting souls for God's glory.
>
> Ellen, have you considered sharing your own narrative, perhaps in both Chinese and English, about your experiences

> balancing professional and family life, guided by your deep faith? Mina's journey is equally compelling. I believe God has blessed both of you with the gift of expression, valuable in both print and speech.

Through our ongoing dialogue, a deep connection was forged, anchored in shared faith and a mutual reverence for the craft of storytelling. Leona extended beyond mere book sharing; she invited us into the sacred practice of writing, highlighting its power to connect and inspire souls.

A WEBINAR BRINGS DEEPER CONNECTIONS

Leona, with a warmth that transcended mere acquaintance, showed an extraordinary interest in our lives, providing both my daughter Mina and me with invaluable guidance.

On April 3, 2021, Mina hosted a webinar on the Chinese Golden Youth platform. The invited speaker was Abigail Xing Wen, a noted author and filmmaker, and our long-time friend from Cleveland, Ohio. As I translated the event, I had shared details with Leona in advance.

To our delight, not only did Mrs. Leona Choy attend our Zoom session, but she also offered us heartening feedback and profound insights. She went a step further by purchasing Abigail's book on Amazon, reading it thoroughly, and sharing a detailed and thoughtful critique with us.

Her compassion and love deeply moved us. Despite her age of 95 and her large family of 10 grandchildren and 13 great-grandchildren, she dedicated a significant amount of time and effort to ministering to us. Receiving such dedicated attention from someone of her stature and wisdom was both an honor and a humbling experience. Our bond grew, evolving into one akin to that of a mother and daughter—so close that I affectionately began to call her Mother Leona.

A NOVICE'S JOURNEY INTO PUBLISHING

In June 2021, the Philadelphia Christian Writers Conference occurred online due to Covid restrictions, drawing numerous Christian writers from nationwide. The event was highlighted by keynote speaker Mother Leona, a revered figure within the Christian literary community.

During her address, Mother Leona delivered a compelling call to action, challenging Christian writers to address the current state of faith in the United States and to advance their missions for the benefit of future generations. At age 96, she was honored with the Christian Writer of the Year award, standing as a stalwart example of Christian commitment and inspiration to us all.

It was Mother Leona who had informed me about this conference and encouraged me to attend. As a novice to the conference, I was making my initial forays into the publishing world. To entice a publisher, I needed to craft a robust book proposal, complete with sample chapters, a project timeline, and an estimated word count, ensuring my book offered a unique perspective in a crowded market. Even before finalizing my first draft, I faced decisions regarding the print run, with costs for producing up to 500 copies of a 60,000-word book ranging from $6,000 to $8,000.

In discussions with various publishers, I discovered that my work, categorized under mission history, confronts challenging market conditions in today's liberal, post-modern environment, exacerbated by rising US-China tensions amid the Ukraine conflict. Despite these obstacles, I am driven by a divine calling and fortified by the support of Mother Leona and my family to persevere in this endeavor.

DIVINE PROVIDENCE IN TIMES OF TRIAL

Our bond was unmistakably shaped by divine providence. Mother Leona, ever the guardian of our family's spiritual and emotional needs, embodied the living testimony of God's active presence in our lives.

On January 1, 2022, Mother Leona reached out to us:

Dear Ellen and Bing and family,

This is the first morning of a new year and the first day of the rest of our lives. It was unusual for me to wake up at 3 am and not fall asleep anymore. Did the Lord want my undivided attention for some reason? Were there people He wanted me to pray for who have asked for my prayers or whose needs I sense? So, I obeyed to pray by name as I listened carefully to His prompting. You are among the people He led me to pray for.

If we were face to face, how would I pray? I found this moving prayer by an unknown intercessor on the link below which I am applying not just for you this morning but for your year ahead. It is about 10 minutes long. I hope you have time to quiet your heart and accept it as what I would pray for you from my heart, if we were together.

https://youtu.be/r8mrfq6SNIU

May you be blessed and guided by the Lord this coming year.

In response, I wrote to Mother Leona on the same day:

Dear Mother Leona:

Your message and the prayer you shared profoundly touched my heart. As my husband and I prayed this morning, the Holy Spirit reminded us of the three recent near misses with calamity, underscoring God's grace in our lives. We are deeply moved by the prayer video, aligning our prayers and resolutions for the new year. You and your family remain in our prayers, revered as beacons during these trying times. Should you need anything, please do not hesitate to reach out. Your influence and guidance are blessings we cherish.

Then Mother Leona wrote back to me:

> Dear "Adopted" Liang family,
>
> I am in awe at how the Lord has protected and guided you and seen you safely through this past month especially. My heart goes out to those with whom you have had grieving encounters and praise God for the way He has brought your family into spiritual unity to face these circumstances together. I believe this is a harbinger of how you can trust Him to guide you through this year no matter what unanticipated situations He will bring into your lives.
>
> There is another specific prayer I have come across which asks God for protection of your home and family: https://youtu.be/3orZrYPCJpQ
>
> Thank you for your prayers for me, for my family as we have mostly recovered from Covid or whatever really is the illness we have been going through, whatever correct or incorrect labels they have been giving the viruses that are a part of normal years during flu seasons. The main leftover from the virus we had seems to be unusual weakness, fatigue, lack of energy which is known to linger for a long time while the immune system struggles to build up again. We are carefully attending to the protocol of specific supplements, medications, and good nutrition.
>
> Grandma Leona

During the difficult days of the pandemic, Mother Leona and her son Rick, who also served as her caregiver, contracted Covid, enduring a very tough recovery. It became evident that God had placed on our hearts a shared calling to support each other through prayer—a deep commitment to seek each other's healing and well-being.

We stayed in touch with Mother Leona through frequent emails and phone calls, wishing we could be there to assist her in person. Eventually, we learned that their relatives and friends rallied to help them through this challenging time. Indeed, God sent angels in human form to aid us, reminding us that we are all His servants, called to heed His guidance attentively.

THE PRECIOUS ENCOUNTER

In March 2022, Bing and I, together with two friends, drove seven hours to visit Mother Leona, spending a delightful and memorable time with her. She was overjoyed to meet us in person, warmly appreciating the beautiful Chinese embroidery we presented as a gift. Radiant and spirited, Mother Leona was deeply immersed in her writing ministry and maintained a vigorous routine, cycling eight miles daily on her indoor bike. Her remarkable determination and boundless affection left us profoundly inspired and touched.

Figure 56: Leona with Ellen in 2022.

THE CZECH APRON FROM PRAGUE

During the summer of 2022, our family visited Prague, the capital city of the Czech Republic and the homeland of Mother Leona. As we wandered through this captivating city, we immersed ourselves in its storied past, reflecting on how Mother Leona had dedicated her life to serve the Chinese, despite her native land's own tumultuous history with religious persecution and political struggles.

In Prague, we bought a Czech apron with a customized print "Leona Choy, Love from Czech" and captured numerous family photos to share with her. For her 97th birthday, we sent this apron along with a delicate Chinese silk scarf. Mother Leona was overjoyed with these gifts. She sent us a photo of herself wearing the Chinese silk scarf

Figure 57: Mother Leona on her 97th birthday in 2022.

and another photo with her granddaughter, little Leona, wearing the Czech apron.

Mother Leona explained the deep cultural significance of an apron in Czech tradition, revealing how it holds a special place in her heart. She shared an article titled "Frantiska's Apron," in which Mother Leona vividly recounts seeking refuge behind her grandmother's apron during shy moments in her childhood. The piece, infused with her deep affection for her grandmother and Czech heritage, moved us profoundly.

GUIDED WITH COMPASSION: MOTHER LEONA'S PERSONAL MENTORSHIP

As the final writing mentee of Mother Leona, I had the honor of her direct mentorship. Despite her fragile health, she remained steadfast in her commitment to coaching me, insisting she was best suited as my mentor given her rich experiences in my writing content. Her warm nurturing felt like a maternal embrace.

Mother Leona was an astute and insightful coach, enhancing my ability to write compellingly about historical subjects. She emphasized the importance of "showing, not telling" to captivate readers and encouraged me to weave a clear, distinct theme throughout my manuscript to differentiate it from other works on the market.

Mother Leona's guidance to pray over my book profoundly shaped my writing process. She introduced me to essential tools like Grammarly and recommended the "Grace for Purpose" YouTube channel for daily spiritual enrichment. Leveraging her extensive network, she connected me with expert editors and publishers and graciously offered me a book contract despite her health challenges.

Mother Leona introduced me to Sarah Lin Lu, a Christian painter and writer. Sarah authored two Chinese books, *Soaring Seeds: Blessings of Early Rain Fellowship in Chengdu* and *Red Leather Suitcase*. With Mother Leona's support, these works were translated into English.

Sarah and I shared a deep passion for the history of AFC, and her painting of the Leaman family at Christiana Lodge of AFC was the initial connection she formed with Mother Leona. From the moment we met, Sarah and I became instant friends, united by our shared spiritual and emotional bond with Mother Leona and our Chinese heritage. Both of us graduated from Nankai University and are very close in age.

Sarah and her husband David guided us to the gravesite where China Mary Leaman, Christiana Tsai, and Lucy Leaman rest together. The gravestone bears the comforting inscription, "Jesus will never leave us." This serene resting place is in the cemetery behind the Presbyterian church near the AFC headquarters in Paradise, PA. Here, too, lie the ancestors of the Leaman family of Leaman Place.

Figure 58: Ellen and Sarah at the burial site of Mary Leaman, Lucy Leaman, and Christiana Tsai.

Standing there, surrounded by the gravestones of the Leamans, filled me with an indescribable sense of history and gratitude. It is through their sacrifice and unwavering dedication to serving the Chinese people that we have come to know Jesus Christ. We are the beneficiaries of their labor, and it is now our responsibility to carry the torch for those who have not yet encountered God and still live in darkness.

In 2022, Sarah informed me about the upcoming retirement ceremony of AFC's President, Rev. David Chow, knowing I was writing a book about AFC's history. Although I had never met Rev. Chow and initially had no plans to attend, the day before the ceremony, I suddenly felt God speaking to me: "How can you write his father's story behind his back? You should go and meet him!" Startled by this divine message, I shared the experience with Bing, who wholeheartedly supported me. That night, we drove through torrential rain, stayed at a hotel along the way, and arrived at AFC the next morning.

Figure 59: Ellen and Bing with Rev. David Chow and his wife Karen in 2022.

Rev. David Chow received us warmly. Later, he generously dedicated a substantial amount of his time to reviewing my manuscript, providing invaluable insights throughout the book. His contribution was very instrumental in the completion of this book.

During that trip, we had hoped to visit Mother Leona, but she had just been released from the hospital and was restricted from receiving visitors under her doctor's orders. Instead, Mother Leona introduced us to Dr. Ivan Leaman, whose ancestors were cousins of the Leaman family of Leaman Place. Along with Sarah and her husband, David Daku, we visited Dr. Ivan Leaman and his wife, Mary Ellen.

Dr. Ivan Leaman, a devoted medical doctor and missionary, spent the first decade of his career serving in Somalia during the 1960s. He authored the book *Born for a Purpose: A Memoir from the Horn of Africa*, a poignant tribute to the Leaman family's spiritual legacy. Our visit with Dr. Leaman and his wife, Mary Ellen, was truly delightful. They regaled us with wonderful stories from their time in Somalia and generously gifted us a cherished copy of his book.

Dr. Ivan's extended research, "The Remarkable Leaman Family of Leaman Place," became an integral part of this book. His work also inspired me to undertake research on Charley and Lucy Leaman, missionaries who went to China and passed away there, leaving a sig-

Figure 60: Bing, Dr. Ivan Leaman, Mary Ellen Leaman, and Ellen in Nov. of 2022.

nificant mark on the Leaman family's legacy. Unfortunately, their life stories are missing from most sources.

With scarce information available, I meticulously examined the historical annual reports of the Board of Foreign Missions of the Presbyterian Church of the US from 1847 to 1920. The findings from this research, combined with Dr. Ivan Leaman's publication, filled all the gaps in the history of the Land of Promise.

THE SEASON OF TRIALS: MOTHER LEONA'S LIFE AT THE LAST STAGE

Mother Leona, in robust health and maintaining a vigorous lifestyle, encountered a significant challenge when she and her son Rick, her primary caregiver, contracted Covid in early December 2021.

As Mother Leona battled the virus, her other son, Cliff, and his wife, Jo, stepped in to help but soon found themselves needing to quarantine due to their own Covid diagnoses. Mother Leona, struggling with fatigue and mobility issues due to pre-existing foot problems, received support from a neighbor who kindly left food outside her door during the Covid time.

Throughout this period, our concern for Mother Leona and her family deepened, and we prayed fervently for their recovery. Thankfully, she gradually began to recuperate, a relief to us all. However, it soon became apparent that she was still suffering from extreme weakness and fatigue post-recovery.

On March 23, 2022, Mother Leona's doctor diagnosed her with heart problems, which contributed to her shortness of breath and tiredness. Her heart's poor pumping ability caused fluid retention, leading to swollen, heavy ankles and legs, affecting her balance and mobility.

Mother Leona adapted her lifestyle, limiting her time sitting and balancing periods of rest with her feet elevated to manage her symptoms. She approached this new regime with a spirit of intentional relaxation, avoiding even the positive stress of prolonged social visits.

On June 22, 2022, Mother Leona celebrated her 97th birthday in seemingly good health. However, just months later, on October 19, she faced a critical situation and was rushed to the emergency room due to a heart complication. Despite these serious circumstances, her resilience shone brightly. Throughout her hospital stay, she engaged with medical staff and patients, sharing her faith and distributing copies of her book, *Hospital Gowns Don't Have Pockets!* as tokens of gratitude.

In her communications, Mother Leona wrote, "I trust the Lord for planting me wherever He wants me whenever. Also, a chance to pray for friends who have shared their own needs with me. All good. Praying for your needs too."

On November 9, 2022, an update from her son Rick described another moment of divine intervention: a scheduled procedure to drain fluid from around her heart was abruptly canceled when the fluid unexpectedly vanished, much to the joy of the medical team. This development brought immense relief and joy to Mother Leona and her family, reinforcing her faith and gratitude toward all those praying for her.

On November 11, 2022, she expressed her sentiments in a poignant message:

> I greatly regret not being able to attend Rev. David Chow's Retirement Event tomorrow. I have been hospitalized for several weeks due to procedures related to my Congestive Heart Failure and lung issues. On behalf of the original Founders, I send my highest commendations to David, thanking God

> for his long and faithful service. I hope the occasion brings together many AFC friends who are bonded but have never met each other. Enjoy the fellowship! I wish I could join you.

Throughout her health challenges, Mother Leona remained an active communicator, maintaining her spiritual and emotional connections with friends, family, and supporters. Her journey underscored her unwavering faith and the strength she derives from her community and her firm belief in God's providence.

EMBRACING GOD'S PLAN AT LIFE'S SUNSET

In the waning light of her earthly journey, Mother Leona wrote two profound letters that reflect the depth of her faith and her serene acceptance of God's sovereign plan. She shared her insights and farewells that transcended the usual fare of correspondence. Her words, steeped in the wisdom of a life devoted to faith, offered a rare glimpse into her soul, even in the face of physical decline, and remained anchored in the promise of divine faithfulness.

On January 18, 2023, Mother Leona wrote:

> Dear Special beloved friends Ellen and Sarah,
>
> I know you wish me well and ask often about my "recovery" and "progress" and pray for my "healing." I do have faith in God's healing. I am so grateful to you. It is not a lack of faith or optimism that I must say what follows. Of course, I believe that Jesus heals today. Nor do I disbelieve the prognosis of my cardiologist and other medical professionals.
>
> The fact is that I am 98 and my mortal body is wearing out (as the Apostle Paul admitted of himself in 2 Cor. 4:16 to 5:1-9). Especially my physical heart is no longer functioning properly. You both had natural mothers whose time came to leave for Heaven. That is in the plan of God.

The fact is, unless God wills a miracle, I am told that I should not expect to "recover" and "get better." We must face this with the JOY that the Lord has ahead for us.

I continue to be very physically weak. That is why I can no longer do editing and writing and publishing as before. The most I can do is pray and work with God's enabling to keep posting and encouraging my many friends through my website blog posts. They, in turn, encourage me by the comments I receive—that what God is giving me to write is really reaching its target, their hearts and life situations.

If it is still in God's big plan that I continue that "for a while longer" "for your sakes," as Paul declared, then I am willing and eager. (Philippians 1:24) "but it is more necessary for you that I remain in the body."

I just wanted you two beloved friends to understand that our expectations must be realistic while you continue to pray for God's will to be done in the rest of my life to please Him.

Do you understand what I am trying to say? I love you both so dearly! You are like my two daughters.

Maminka (Mother) Leona

On January 20, 2023, Mother Leona wrote:

Dear Ellen, (and Bing) (and also to Sarah and David),

Concerning your urging me to pursue the STORYCORPS. I appreciate your kind intentions and encouragement that I record my life story for permanence in this manner—in an interview fashion—with family members asking the questions. I do not believe this suits my particular situation. It would work better for someone who was not already a lifetime writer and has written several memoirs already. In my case, it seems redundant. In my lifetime of writing and publishing up to the present I have already covered what I would wish to say as to my legacy and view and philosophy of life. My Christian faith, experience, and witness. I would have nothing new to reveal.

That in itself is reason enough not to expend my energy to do STORYCORPS.

But there are other factors: My age and permanent limitations on my health. These are not excuses. I am not in a "recovering" stage whereby I would look forward to "becoming better." I must live within the limitations of energy that I possess. I have a certain amount of energy to invest. With God's enabling and taking the medications necessary to maintain life. In particular, my deteriorating physical heart is giving out. This is an undeniable fact. My diagnosis and prognosis are CONGESTIVE HEART FAILURE which is progressive and symptoms are predictable. I don't feel that God is asking me to write all over again in some other format or speak that which I have already written and recorded or spoken. I don't have that extra energy to call upon.

That doesn't mean that I don't believe in healing miracles. I do, if God requires it. In this case, I don't believe that He does. By all means, I want to do God's will. I also want you to understand my position. I hope you will let me know that you understand.

Always with my love. I am honored that both of your families are like my own, a part of my very life, not as if you were "adopted."

Maminka/Mother Leona

Mother Leona's messages serve as a profound testimony to the strength of her unwavering faith. Her acceptance of life's twilight not as a defeat but as a fulfillment of God's plan reveals a heart fully surrendered to God's timing and purposes. These messages teach us that true faith involves trusting in God's sovereignty over every aspect of our lives and finding joy in the assurance of His eternal promises.

They remind us that even in our final chapters, we are called to reflect God's love and to live out the faith we profess, making every moment an offering to Him, until we are called home.

A VOICE FOR THE VOICELESS: SPEAKING AT HER MEMORIAL SERVICE

Mother Leona, to me, was nothing short of a guardian angel dispatched by the divine. Compelled by a profound connection, I felt a strong urge to attend her memorial service, pay my respects, and connect with her family in person. I am deeply thankful for Bing's unwavering support and his willingness to join me on the lengthy drive.

Figure 61: Ellen spoke at Mother Leona's Memorial Service.

Our bond, divinely orchestrated, seemed to transcend the confines of time and space, binding our spirits whether on earth or beyond.

As we embarked on our seven-hour journey, Bing proposed that I should share my gratitude for Mother Leona during the service. Initially, the thought was daunting to me. Given her stature as a venerated Christian leader and the presence of many distinguished guests and online audience, I questioned my place to speak. Yet, as I turned to prayer, I felt a clear directive from God to share my thoughts. The more I prayed, the clearer and more insistent this calling became. Reluctantly yet resolutely, I chose to heed God's call.

On the morning of March 13, 2023, as we drove to the service, I practiced my speech repeatedly. Upon arrival, during a brief coffee break, we met Mother Leona's family. Despite having only previously met her son, Rick, I immediately felt a profound connection with many of her family members, especially her eldest grandson Pastor Ed Choy who was the host of the memorial service.

Entering the service venue and catching sight of Mother Leona's casket, emotions welled up within me, reinforcing the deep spiritual connection that felt fated by God, transcending her physical absence.

The service atmosphere was reverent and I sensed the presence of the Lord. So, I prayed, "God, let your words flow through me. Let me be your vessel, speaking only what you want me to say."

The service, led by Mother Leona's grandson Pastor Ed Choy, struck a balance between solemnity and lighthearted remembrance. Following heartfelt tributes from her family members and a touching homage by Mr. Paul Tseng, honoring Mother Leona's extraordinary contribution to founding AFC, I approached the podium.

Standing there, the words that flowed from me were not those I had rehearsed but rather those God placed upon my heart in that moment. As I stepped down from the stage, I couldn't recall exactly what I had said. Yet, upon watching the replay, I realized I had spoken eloquently, conveying the deep gratitude of the Chinese community for the Choy family's enduring dedication and faithfulness.

God had indeed spoken through me, turning my initial reluctance into a testament of faith. It was a moment of pure grace, a profound indication that we are but instruments of His will, crafted to fulfill divine purposes far beyond our own intentions.

DREAMS THROUGH GENERATIONS

In 2017, during the ribbon-cutting and dedication ceremony of the Christiana Tsai Memorial Lodge, Mother Leona delivered a remarkable speech titled "Dreams through Generations." This speech, later included in her book *Curtain Call from the Dark Chamber*, resonated deeply with the theme God had placed in my heart.

Mother Leona's profound words, "We are all instruments of God, and God is realizing His vision and plan through us across many gen-

Figure 62: The air view of AFC's Great Commission Training Center in 2022.

erations," underscored God's call for individuals from diverse eras to fulfill His divine purposes.

The narrative began with Peter Leman, who journeyed from Europe in 1717 and acquired a tract of land known as "the Land of Promise." This land was part of Penn's vision to create a new world valuing individual rights, religious tolerance, and democracy.

Over the centuries, God mobilized many, including Charles and Lucy Leaman, Mary A. and Lucy A. Leaman, Christiana Tsai, Rev. Ted and Leona Choy, and Rev. Moses Chow, along with countless missionaries, to propagate the gospel globally. Their collective dedication led to the donation of the Leamans' land to AFC, an organization tasked with spreading the gospel among Chinese intellectuals worldwide.

This once modest acorn has matured into a mighty oak, its branches extending far and wide, sheltering and nurturing faith across the globe.

As children of God, our role is to remain steadfast and obedient, trusting that He will empower us to achieve His purposes. Though His plans are beyond our comprehension, and we are merely fragments of a vast mosaic, it is only when God assembles all the pieces that the complete picture emerges. Through His sovereign revelation, we gradually perceive the grandeur of His plan.

May we each strive to be faithful servants of God. And when we finally stand before Him, may He greet us with the words, "Well done, my faithful servant. Now come and enjoy the feast with Me in heaven." Let our lives contribute to God's eternal design, ensuring our efforts resonate through generations.

As we reflect and connect the dots of missionary lives, we see a divine symphony, with notes played by His faithful servants, their lives dedicated to His glory. We feel the presence of the Lord, leading and guiding those who are willing to listen and obey, offering their lives as living sacrifices.

God's plan is beyond our comprehension, yet for those who choose to obey, He offers heavenly peace and joy, regardless of their physical conditions or material possessions. These servants focus on heaven rather than earthly matters, and God rewards them abundantly, not only in heaven but through the lasting impact of their deeds on earth.

They have built with precious metals, not hay, following God's divine blueprint, creating legacies that eclipse their earthly existence. Their works, beyond their wildest imaginations, will be remembered forever. Every soul woven into the tapestry of this story, every life chronicled within the Mosaic of Divine Symphony, shares a singular purpose: to obey God, to bring Him honor, and by His grace, to glorify Him so that all nations might come to know Him. As children of God, we are embraced by His unwavering faithfulness. As devoted followers, we shall never stray from His will. May all generations exalt His goodness and greatness, proclaiming His name so that every nation under heaven may come to know the Lord. To God be the glory, forever and ever. Amen.

EPILOGUE:

THE SPIRITUAL JOURNEY OF THE LIANGS

A JOURNEY OF RESILIENCE, FAITH, AND HEALING

Bing Liang

MY FAMILY BACKGROUND

I was born in 1960, in Jinan, Shandong Province. My father, Yanfu Liang (梁延綒, 1928-1988), served as a military officer, while my mother, Meiqing Cong (从梅卿, 1929-2003), dedicated her life to teaching music at a local high school. I grew up in a small coastal village, where my childhood unfolded along the shores, with the rhythmic crash of waves and the cries of gulls as the backdrop to my days. My favorite pastime was catching crabs beneath the rocks and collecting seashells scattered along the sand—a passion I shared with my dad. Sometimes, I enjoyed a quiet moment sitting on the beach, gazing out as ships sailed across the horizon where the sea and sky meet, imagining the world that lay beyond the sea.

Figure 1: Bing in college in 1982.

But as the tides of my childhood ebbed, a darker current swept through the nation—the Cultural Revolution. It was a time of upheaval and hardship, and in the midst of this storm, my maternal grandmother became our steadfast anchor. She cared for me and my two sisters, sheltering us from the worst of the turmoil as best she could.

A JOURNEY OF RESILIENCE

At the age of 16, like many of my peers, I was sent to the countryside as part of the government's movement to have "educated youth" re-educated by the poor and lower-middle class peasants. In a distant and humble village, we labored daily in the fields, enduring the unrelenting demands of physical toil. We lived in a communal camp, far away from the warmth and comfort of our homes and families. Yet, in the midst of these trials, the quiet seeds of resilience were sown deep within us.

In 1976, Mao Zedong's passing away marked a pivotal shift in China's political landscape. Under Deng Xiaoping's leadership, the national college entrance exam was reinstated in December 1977, following a decade-long suspension during the Cultural Revolution (1966-1976). This change rekindled hope for millions of young people, reopening their path to higher education.

It felt as though a long-closed door had suddenly swung open. After months of grueling work at the intellectual youth camp, I immersed myself in intense study, with my entire family supporting me by gathering study materials. I was driven by a deep desire to flee from what seemed like a hopeless future.

By God's grace, I was fortunate to be among the first group to pass the national college exams, securing a place at the prestigious Shandong College of Oceanography, now known as China Ocean University, where I was assigned to study maritime meteorology. After graduation, I was offered a teaching position at Dalian Maritime College, which has since become Dalian Maritime University.

Though I was grateful for the opportunity to teach, a quiet restlessness began to stir within me. Though the study of maritime meteorology was fulfilling, it left me with lingering questions, especially in the challenging field of weather forecasting. My curiosity deepened, and soon I was drawn to the fields of economics and statistics, spending countless hours in independent study. I lost track of how many metal pots I burned while absorbed in studying, distracted even while cooking noodles.

This determination eventually led me to take the entrance exam for the Academia Sinica Institute of Applied Mathematics. I passed and pursued a master's degree in applied statistics, which opened my eyes to new realms of understanding.

Those three years in Beijing were deeply transformative, not only because of the academic knowledge I gained but also for the personal blessings that unfolded. It was there that I met Ellen, the girl who would become my wife, and her love and companionship have been a blessing ever since.

A JOURNEY OF AMBITION, HARD WORK, AND SUCCESS

On Nov 26, 1988, my family entrusted me with their entire life savings to purchase a one-way ticket to the United States. I arrived with just $40, two suitcases, and a heart full of dreams and determination. Thankfully, Ellen had arrived about 100 days earlier than me at the same university.

Figure 2: Bing and Ellen got married in 1989.

On August 22, 1989, we were married by Pastor Jason Chen, the university chaplain. Though we weren't Christians at the time, we chose a pastor and the university chapel for our ceremony to embrace a Western-style wedding. Yet, despite our lack of faith, God has blessed our marriage. Two years later, our son Reece was born at Mercy Hospital.

After earning my second master's degree in Quality Management and Productivity, a deeper ambition began to grow within me, inspiring me to embark on a new journey. With courage, I made the bold decision to shift my career focus to finance. This choice ultimately led me to pursue a doctoral degree at the University of Iowa. It was there that my career entered an extraordinary new chapter, opening doors to a world completely new to me. After five years of rigorous study and persevering through numerous challenges, I earned my Ph.D. in finance.

In 1995, I started my journey as an assistant professor at Case Western Reserve University in Cleveland, Ohio. Through hard work and self-discipline, I convinced myself that I was the master of my destiny, capable of achieving anything I set my mind to. I had realized the American Dream—thriving in my career, with a loving family, a son, and a home. I emerged as one of the early pioneers in hedge fund research. Yet in my pride, I dismissed every attempt others made to share the Gospel with me. But God, in His gentle wisdom and with a sense of humor, knew exactly how to reach my heart.

THE JOURNEY OF FAITH

I met Sister Huiqing at a Chinese community event. Remarkably, her hometown was just about a mile from the village where I had lived at the communal youth camp. She warmly invited us to a gathering at her home. After a delicious dinner, we realized it was a Bible study group. Although my wife and I weren't actively seeking faith at the time and were even somewhat resistant, the discussions intrigued us. Week after week, we found ourselves returning. What initially seemed like a chance encounter became the starting point of our family's faith journey.

What we didn't realize was that, from that moment on, Sister Huiqing began praying for our family every day as she passed our house on her way to work, answering God's call. God had placed a burden on her heart, revealing that He had a purpose for our family in His kingdom. Faithful in God's calling, she not only mentored our family but also grew into the role of pastor. Today, she leads a flourishing online megachurch, ministering to over 1,000 people and guiding a dedicated team of prayer warriors and servants of God, offering spiritual support and guidance to countless others.

After a few years of Bible study and regular church attendance, both my wife and son accepted Christ and were ready for baptism. Despite their encouragement, along with Sister Huiqing's, I didn't feel called to follow. I believed I was a good person—diligent and generous. Yet, as I faced life's challenges, the Holy Spirit revealed my sins and pride, showing me I couldn't save myself and needed God's cleansing.

At a Thanksgiving Christian conference in Chicago in 2000, Pastor Che Ahn delivered a powerful message that stirred me deeply. When he invited seekers to accept Christ, I found myself walking forward to the stage, as if guided by an unseen force. The following day, on November 26, 2000—exactly 12 years after I had arrived in the U.S.—my wife, son, unborn daughter Mina, and I were baptized in the jacuzzi at the conference hotel of Chicago.

As we drove back to Cleveland, a Bible verse filled my heart: "Therefore, if anyone is in Christ, the new creation has come: The old has gone, the new is here!" (2 Corinthians 5:17). An overwhelming sense of joy and freedom swept over me, knowing that God had cleansed me of my sins and made me a new person in Christ.

A PROFOUND SPIRITUAL ENCOUNTER

The joy of receiving the Gospel ignited in me a deep passion to share the good news with everyone I encountered—neighbors, students, colleagues, cab drivers, barbers, businessmen, and even massage therapists. Naturally, I started with my own family, beginning with my mother. One year after my baptism, and through my influence and help from the local church, she accepted Christ, and her faith brought new light to her later years. She became radiant with joy, dedicating much of her time to leading church choirs. After a long battle with cancer, she peacefully went home to be with the Lord.

On May 14, 2003, my mother's birthday—the same day she departed from this world—I experienced a profound spiritual touch from God. That year, despite traveling to China four times to be by her side, even in the midst of the SARS epidemic, I had to return to the U.S. for my duties as a finance professor. On that day, I was flying to Washington, D.C., to testify before the Securities and Exchange Commission (SEC) as an expert witness on hedge fund regulations. Just before boarding, I received a call from Ellen, sharing that my sister had said our mother could be called to the Lord at any moment. As the plane ascended above the clouds, I witnessed a breathtaking sunset, and an overwhelming sense of heavenly peace filled my heart.

As the plane touched down, I called my sister in China and learned that my mother had passed away on her birthday—at the very moment when God had filled my heart with peace high above the clouds. In that instant, I knew she was in God's arms, and a profound sense of peace and relief washed over me. That peace remained with me as I confidently delivered my testimony at the SEC meeting, which was broadcast publicly. Through it all, I felt God's comforting presence, strengthening me every step of the way.

The following year, I returned to China to lay my parents' ashes to rest together. As I walked through the green fields toward their grave by the sea, Psalm 23 came to mind: "The Lord is my shepherd; I shall not want. He makes me lie down in green pastures; He leads me beside still waters." These beautiful words are now inscribed on their tombstone.

For over 20 years, I've had the privilege of leading many family members and students to Christ. With passion and dedication, I've faithfully served God both in my local church and beyond—as a deacon chair, short-term missionary, preacher, Bible study leader, and adult Sunday school teacher. I've also had the honor of preaching at the New England Winter Student (NEWS) camp on multiple occasions, as well as in several churches across the nation.

Alongside my family and co-workers, I've embarked on about ten missionary trips to the Chinese Overseas Christian Mission (COCM) in the UK, where I preached at their year-end family/student camps and actively served in their ministry.

Every time I serve the Lord, I am filled with a deep, abiding joy that sustains and inspires me. My family and I were blessed with the opportunity to return to the Chicago hotel where we were all baptized, and each time, I couldn't help but sing the timeless hymn, "Amazing Grace."

Amazing grace! how sweet the sound,
 That saved a wretch; like me!
I once was lost, but now am found,
 Was blind, but now I see.

THE SACRED DELIVERANCE

On November 30, 2020, during my daily devotional with my devotion group, a verse from Luke 8:43-44 struck me deeply: "And a woman was there who had been subject to bleeding for twelve years, but no one could heal her. She came up behind him (Jesus) and touched the edge of his cloak, and immediately her bleeding stopped." The phrase "twelve years" resonated with me profoundly, as it mirrored the exact duration that I had been dependent on a breathing machine for sleep apnea. At that moment, a spark of faith was ignited within me—I believed that I, too, could be healed. From then on, this newfound conviction would cause me to tremble in prayer, and it became a frequent occurrence during family prayers, even before meals.

After over 30 days of experiencing this trembling, I felt a divine urgency for healing but sensed an unseen bondage holding me back. My wife Ellen helped me to reach out to Pastors Rhema Ma and Pastor David Du, whom we had met at Agape Renewal Ministry in California during a Christian conference. Both are known for their healing gifts. On January 18, 2021—Martin Luther King Day—they conducted a long healing session for me over Zoom.

Figure 3: Reece, Mina, Ellen, and Bing at the end of fasting in 2021.

After the session, I felt a release. For the first time in 12 years, I napped and then slept through the night without my breathing machine, although I did wake up with mild discomfort. Over the following nights, I began experiencing increasing headaches, sometimes so severe that painkillers couldn't help. But through it all, my faith remained steadfast.

Figure 4: Bing said goodbye to the breathing machine in 2021.

Seeking further guidance, I contacted Pastor David again, and he recommended fasting. I began fasting at noon on a Thursday, and Ellen joined me the next morning. Reece and Mina started fasting on Saturday, and so was the church pastor. United in spirit, our entire family fasted for five days, consuming only water, juice, and other liquids. Mina extended her fast to seven days, astonishing us all with her faith and resolve. By the end of the fasting, each of us had lost between 5 and 8 pounds.

This was our first extended spiritual fast as a family, and it drew us closer together, deepening our faith and spiritual sensitivity. Remarkably, my minor health issues began to clear up during the fast, and profound personal revelations surfaced. Most notably, my headaches diminished significantly, and by the end of the seven days, my overnight oxygen levels averaged 96%—a level typical of healthy individuals. We celebrated this incredible recovery as a significant milestone in my journey. I even wrote a testimony titled "Saying Goodbye to the Breathing Machine," featuring a photo of the equipment that had accompanied me worldwide for over a decade, now rendered unnecessary. The article was published by the Chinese Christian Mission magazine in October 2021.

Our fast not only facilitated a miraculous healing but also brought us into a deeper connection with God's presence. Inspired by this transformative experience, we have committed to fasting regularly, seeking to maintain this closeness with God while nurturing our physical, emotional, and spiritual health.

A BI-VOCATIONAL VIEW

In 2021, my service at the church became particularly challenging. As the chair of the deacon board, I coordinated with the board and assisted the pastor in managing the church, with many responsibilities to handle during the pandemic. After my term as a deacon ended, I spent time in quiet reflection before God, seeking to equip myself so I could rise again like an eagle. During this period of searching, I came across Teacher Roger Kung's course, To Be the First and to Be Only (Teacher Kung was the Board Chair of Ambassador for Christ at the time), and I immediately enrolled. The vision of this course resonated deeply with my pursuit of a holistic life, where faith, work, and life are in balance.

I realized that I had been constrained by the dualism of the "sacred-secular divide," which separates life into two realms: the sacred (spiritual) and the secular (worldly). This divide implies that activities like worship and prayer are part of the sacred realm, while work and social activities belong to the secular. I came to understand that this division is artificial. Instead, we should embrace a more integrated view where every aspect of life—whether sacred or secular—can be lived out in faith and service to God.

After completing the course, I was grateful to join Roger's coaching team, where I had the opportunity to learn, practice, and exchange ideas with other coaches from diverse churches and professional backgrounds. Over the past few years, I have taken three additional courses from Roger, and several called-to-work courses from Elder Elaine Kung, each of which has significantly broadened my perspective and enhanced my capacity to serve. With Pastor David Wang's support, we have also introduced a Sunday school program at our church focused on bi-vocational ministry.

Looking back, I see God's hand guiding me through every season. What began as a quest for success became a journey of faith, as God transformed my hardships and ambitions into a story of grace and redemption. Today, my greatest joy is serving Him, sharing the good news, and witnessing His work among others. Through every challenge, I am reminded of His faithfulness and move forward with gratitude, trusting that His plans are far greater than my own. From me, four generations of Christians now stand in my family, a living testament to God's promise: "But showing love to a thousand generations of those who love me and keep my commandments" (Deuteronomy 5:10).

PLANTED BY THE STREAM

Reece Liang

Figure 5: Reece in 1995.

Have you ever asked yourself, "Why am I a Christian?" or perhaps "Why am I not a Christian?" Have you asked yourself recently? Thinking on my own testimony this morning, I hoped for a single word answer or a few punchy lines but I could only think of my journey so far. Perhaps that is why the Bible is full of stories, some feelings can only be expressed through the richness of a story. Truth really is stranger than fiction. I would describe my journey so far as a transition from obligation to understanding, and now, to a place of deep gratitude.

I grew up in a Christian household, baptized when I was 10 years old. Much of my developed memory is filled with running around in church with friends after Sunday school, and as a teenager reluctantly getting out of bed on Sundays but enjoying time spent with youth group friends. Up until college, I went to church because that's where my friends were and that's just what our family did. During the weekdays, I lived what I would characterize as a pretty rebellious high school experience and during the weekends, I went to church. This bifurcated life carried into college where on the one hand I was a seasoned Christian—I knew the stories and the language—but on the other hand I did what everybody around me was doing and more, experiencing what I believed to be the full spectrum of life.

Figure 6: Reece graduated from London Business School in 2021.

It wasn't until my first few years out of college that my two lives began to catch up with me. My theology began to show signs of cracking. The ritualistic attendance of church was no longer enough to overcome my behavior the other six days of the week. Church began to feel heavy. I felt constantly guilty. I began to doubt, and I knew something was wrong. My behavior indicated I was a committed Christian, going to church on Sundays and as many Bible studies on Wednesdays as I could. But my heart didn't want God, it wanted the pleasures of this life. My life didn't feel consistent, it didn't feel real and something had to give.

I consciously and subconsciously began to look for answers: I started journaling, exercised more, read self-help books, began seeing a therapist, and leaned heavily into my relationships at the time. These activities provided a sense of support, and in many ways they did, but they were never enough. Sometimes things felt better, other times they felt worse, and on the whole it just felt like I was going in circles. During this time, I never stopped going to church and even though my private life didn't feel very "Christian", I just kept going. Like my other activities, it sometimes provided a sense of healing and other times not.

I don't remember the exact moment or context I had this realization, perhaps it was when I was thinking of what self-help book to read next (I've always loved to read), but it was pivotal for me. I realized that I had never actually thought of the Bible as a place where there might be answers. For all the books I'd read, I couldn't say I had actually read the Bible in its entirety. I had been going to church for over 10 years and despite hearing snippets through sermons and Sunday schools, I had never actually read the Bible - not chronologically, not as a volume that might contain helpful information, not in any capacity outside of a mandated one. In my heart, I'm not sure I had even held the Bible to the same esteem as Dale Carnegie's *How to Win Friends and Influence People*, at least not with regards to applicability to my own life.

Because the Bible can be challenging to read, I began to read books about the Bible. I read Rick Warren's *Purpose Driven Life,* I listened voraciously to Tim Keller's Gospel in Life Podcasts on long drives. I began to take the Bible seriously; I began to take the initiative to try and understand the Bible on my own. This pursuit has completely changed my life. I began to understand the Bible, and I started developing a personal relationship with God. My religion turned into relationship and that has become the bedrock of my faith. I began to knock rather than to stand at the door and hope for it to be opened. What I found has been indescribable. What I found was everything I had been looking for and more. My first love and my last love, the motivation to sit here and write to you today.

Oftentimes we hear of the dramatic life changes, the fantastic stories of overnight change. Mine has taken place across nearly 20 years and continues today. I still battle with a bifurcated life. But knowing Jesus, having a relationship with God, has given me the courage and desire to merge my lives into one, and the change that has taken place is more than I could have ever mustered up myself. The Bible says, the kingdom of heaven is like a mustard seed, though it is the smallest of all seeds, yet when it grows, it is the largest of garden plants and becomes a tree, so that the birds come and perch in its branches. Whether on the outside you look like a patch of dirt, a lanky tree with a few leaves, or a sturdy oak, where you are only you and God truly know. May you be planted by streams of water, which yields its fruit in season and may whatever you do prosper.

LEAP OF FAITH: THREADS OF GOD'S MASTERPIECE

Mina Liang

If I couldn't see or feel God's hand moving in my life, I would have a difficult time calling myself a sincere Christian.

I'm the type of person who can easily get caught up in the weeds of life's trials and tribulations: I relate a lot to the apostle Peter who starts sinking into the ocean the moment he gets overwhelmed. Those close to me know that I always manage to keep myself busy—and usually stressed—by diving headfirst into some new assignment, experience, or goal. Knowing these tendencies that I have, I can say with gratitude that God has been incredibly faithful to me: speaking to me in each new season with guidance and insight and using times of uncertainty to remind me of His omnipotence and goodness.

Like many Christians raised by devout parents, my faith journey began in childhood, shaped by a natural familiarity with Bible stories. But by my mid-teens, I realized that my faith needed to be rebuilt in a deeper, more personal way. I feel incredibly blessed that throughout my young adult years, God has placed mentors, friends, and spiritual experiences in my life at just the right moments. It's been so clear to me that the good things I have aren't the result of my own intellect or effort, but a reflection of His goodness and perfect will for my life.

GAP YEAR 1: PAGEANTS, SCHOOLS AND STARTUPS

There have been multiple times when I have prayed for physical signs, and God has answered in ways that were very clear to me. One particular decision I struggled with was deciding whether to take a year off from school during the COVID-19 pandemic. I had just finished my first year at Swarthmore College and was poised to begin the next semester as a transfer sophomore at Columbia University. But when Columbia announced that classes would be held on Zoom for the year, I felt a strong nudge in my heart to delay my entrance. The problem was, without a solid plan to present to my family for how I'd spend that year off, they weren't on board with the idea. Uncertain about the decision without my family's support, I turned to God, asking Him to confirm what I already sensed was the right decision.

On August 18, 2020—the day before I had to give Columbia my decision—my family and I took a short trip to New Hampshire. Standing at the peak of Mount Washington, I breathed in the crisp wind that followed a passing thunderstorm. My parents had parked our car near a lookout point that was supposed to offer a view of multiple mountain range peaks that stood within the presidential mountain range. But instead of the sweeping vista I expected, all I could see was a thick wall of gray clouds left over from the storm, completely hiding the mountains except for the tree-covered green bases at the bottom.

As I stared at the clouds, I prayed: "God, if I'm right about my intuition, give me a sign: Show me the tip of one of these mountains." In the next moment, a small gap in the clouds formed, revealing a patch of blue sky. I watched as the clouds continued to part even more, forming a small round window that moved with the clouds themselves, showing first the sky, and then the outline of a mountain edge. I knew at that moment that I was watching God answer my prayer, but I still gasped when the window steadily moved until it rested on the mountaintop—a perfect window framing the triangular tip of the mountain peak.

Figure 7: Mina at Mt. Washington in 2020

God gave me exactly the sign I had asked for—something that seemed so small on the outside but was so personal and deliberately aligned with my prayer. After the moment had passed, I ran towards the car, laughing in relief at God's faithfulness and brilliant sense of humor. I shared with my parents what had happened and they were in awe of God's faithfulness as well. I still remember that feeling of triumph in knowing that God had confirmed my desires firsthand with a sign I knew was meant for me. It would be the first of many times in which I would ask God for signs that when He answered, I felt giddy knowing the God of the universe was speaking directly to me.

My gap year surpassed all of our expectations. I led my first start-up, ReneCycle, selling smart-lock technology for bikeshare systems to university campuses across the country. With funding and recognition from top competitions including Y-Combinator, Columbia Venture Competition (CVC), and Penn Climate Ventures, we successfully piloted our anti-theft technology on a pilot program at Swarthmore College. The entire process deeply challenged my business and leadership acumen, spearheading a lifelong passion for advising and working with high-growth businesses.

It was during this time that I also competed for my first Miss America local, earning me the title of Miss Blackstone Valley, which kickstarted my journey into pageantry. Having signed up for my first competition on a complete whim, I never could have foreseen what a long-term impact the program would have on my future and development.

Finally, I had the privilege of serving as the youngest trustee board member at the Pioneer Valley Chinese Immersion Charter School (PVCICS), the elementary school I attended from kindergarten through third grade. This honor was particularly meaningful for me, since this was the school I had attended before being homeschooled for 5 years and then attending Deerfield Academy. Becoming a board member at the very school which had become such an inflection point for my academic path felt to be almost too perfect of a full-circle moment: reaffirming that the entire trajectory of my homeschool journey was part of God's plan.

A PAGEANT AND A NEW FRIEND

The night before the 2023 Miss Manhattan pageant, I was in an anxious frenzy, unsure if I should even compete. It was 12 hours before I was supposed to arrive at the pageant, and I didn't have an evening gown, talent costume, or any confidence about the task ahead. I had competed in the same local pageant two years prior, but coming back felt like an entirely new challenge: My insecurities from my previous performance resurfaced, and I began to spiral—doubting whether I had what it took to win another title. Part of my anxieties were also rooted in the fact that I had come to realize that despite being in New York City for two years, I was still missing a sense of home or family. I had many friends at school but I struggled with loneliness; I could perform a brave face for others, but I was missing a support system of people with whom I felt I didn't always have to be funny, cool, or strong.

Figure 8: Mina won the first runner-up in the Miss New York Competition 2024.

One friend that I had just met from the start of classes a week prior responded to my desperate text for wardrobe help, offering that I come to her apartment to try on dresses she had worn in her own pageants. One of them fit me perfectly, and she even offered to come to my room to help me practice my walk. We ended up just sitting on my floor—as I was at the brink of tears struggling with my swirling thoughts of inadequacy, she poured love and encouragement into me. She gently instructed me to focus on one task at a time, helping me identify a dress from my closet that would serve as my talent costume and asking me probing questions about how I'd present my platform on stage.

She came to my pageant that evening, and I had to blink away tears when she and I locked eyes during that moment when I was crowned for the Miss Liberty title—all while standing in her red gown. This friend—Candice Liang—would become like a sister to me. Already sharing the same last name, and soon we would also share sleepovers, dreams, family members and living spaces with each other. She reignited my pride in my Chinese heritage, helped me embrace unique gifts as a woman, and taught me to love myself more fully. Nine months later, she was by my side when I placed 2nd at Miss New York, but our friendship means far more to me than any pageant title. The night before the Miss Manhattan competition, I begged God to help me find a home in NYC, and when I had none of the wardrobe or preparation I needed, God opened the door for a lifelong friend to walk into my life.

GAP YEAR 2: HOME, MEDIA, AND MICROLENDING

I write this testimony marveling at God's hand in my life while standing before the uncertain future of yet another gap year I was called to take following my graduation from Columbia. Going against the advice from my family, industry, and society, I took a leap of faith into yet another year of delaying my life without a real proposal for the road ahead. Since graduating, I've placed first runner-up at the Miss New York competition, traveled solo through seven states, and deepened my understanding of my parents and my hometown, Amherst—discovering meaning and purpose in ways I never expected. Additionally, I am preparing for a mission trip to Zambia with my family.

And yet, I have never felt more peace or joy in my life. I used to show up to church, hoping that God would solve my immediate problems, but I've learned that trusting Him also means being patient and allowing His will to unfold over time. I know that God is the master weaver, and His plan is so intricate—filled with unimaginable intention and specificity—that our lives will manifest their full meaning only when we surrender control to the creator of the universe.

THE MASTER OF THE MOSAIC

I imagine that my mother felt a similar—if not much larger—tug in her heart when she surrendered the corporate career she had so painstakingly labored for, following God's will for her to return home. I imagine her own uncertainty was tantamount when she decided to take my schooling into her own hands—a five-year commitment that would fundamentally define the course of my life and my family's love and bond for one another. I imagine that our lives will continually be characterized by the leaps of faith that God asks us to take: at the time, we may not be able to fully explain our decision, but over time their purpose will be made clear.

God works in ways mysterious to our own comprehension. The brilliance of His plan is far too intricate for any one person to predict or appreciate. When we submit ourselves to God's will, we let our lives be puzzle pieces for a vision far greater than ourselves. Only when we string together narratives across generations can we appreciate the beauty of the Master's mosaic. The best we can do is to position our hearts to welcome His presence, seek for wisdom to interpret His instructions, and ask for the courage we need to execute our small parts.

The rest is in His hands!

"Ask and it will be given to you; seek and you will find; knock and the door will be opened to you. For everyone who asks receives; the one who seeks finds; and to the one who knocks, the door will be opened. (Matthew 7:7-8)